DESIGNER NEEDLEPOINT

25 Exclusive Designs from the Royal School of Needlework to Kaffe Fassett and Susan Duckworth

Edited by Hugh Ehrman

CENTURY

London Melbourne Auckland Johannesburg

Also available from Century
DESIGNER KNITTING by HUGH EHRMAN

First published in 1987 by Century Hutchinson Ltd,
Brookmount House, 62-65 Chandos Place,
Covent Garden, London WC2N 4NW

Century Hutchinson Australia Pty Ltd,
PO Box 496, 16-22 Church Street, Hawthorn,
Victoria 3122, Australia

Century Hutchinson New Zealand Ltd,
PO Box 40-086, Glenfield, Auckland 10,
New Zealand

Century Hutchinson South Africa Pty Ltd,
PO Box 337, Bergvlei, 2012 South Africa

Reprinted 1987

British Library Cataloguing in Publication Data
Designer needlepoint: 25 exclusive designs
    from the Victoria and Albert Museum and
    the Royal School of Needlework to Kaffe
    Fassett.
    1. Canvas embroidery——Patterns
    I. Ehrman, Hugh
    746.44'2041   TT778.C3
    ISBN 0-7126-1470-2

Photography: Belinda Banks
Art Direction and Styling: Gabi Tubbs
Additional Photography: Nic Barlow

Film set by SX Composing Ltd, Rayleigh, Essex
Printed and bound in Great Britain by
Hazell, Watson and Viney Ltd, Aylesbury

CONTENTS

PREFACE   4

INTRODUCTION by Eleanor Van Zandt   5

ROYAL SCHOOL OF NEEDLEWORK   17

Victorian Bird   Paradise Bird   Honeysuckle Chair Seat   Floral Footstool
Trellis and Butterfly Footstool   Chippendale Rose

SUSAN DUCKWORTH   39

Oakleaves and Acorns   Urns and Fruits

SUSANNA LISLE   49

Chintz

EMBROIDERERS' GUILD   55

Fox and Crane   Turkish Stripe   Red House

SUSAN SKEEN   69

Three Birds   Shells   Seashore Garland

EDWIN BELCHAMBER   83

Lily Pond   Walled Garden

VICTORIA AND ALBERT MUSEUM   91

Carnations   Elephant   The Harvesters   Vase Rug

KAFFE FASSETT   109

Seabird   Peony Jar   Esphahan Rose   Baroda Stripe

ACKNOWLEDGEMENTS   126

ORDER FORM FOR KITS   127

PREFACE

It is now nine years since Ehrman produced their first tapestry kit, 'Caucasian Flower' by Kaffe Fassett, and over those years we have amassed a rich collection of designs from a wide variety of sources. All the tapestries were originally designed to be worked in simple half-cross stitch and the wool quantities for the kits were calculated accordingly. This book has given us the opportunity to present all the designs in chart form, so that more adventurous stitches may be used and the designs themselves may be adapted to the individual embroiderer's requirements.

Eleanor Van Zandt, in her admirable introduction, not only explains how to translate the designs to canvas, how to alter their scale and how to stretch, mount and finish the completed tapestries, but also describes the variety of different stitches that can be used and the context in which they would be most appropriate.

Beside each design you will find suggestions for its adaptation, and possibilities for other ways in which it could be used. Often a border or motif can be extracted from the overall picture and repeated or expanded to make a lovely design on its own. This has been a particularly rewarding section of the book to do. The tapestries featured tend to be densely patterned and coloured, so the scope for simplification and alteration of this kind is tremendous. A Kaffe Fassett cushion, for example, will probably have in it enough separate motifs to support ten different tapestries.

For those who discover patterns they would like to stitch exactly as they are illustrated, the kits, including the printed canvas and all the Appleton tapestry wool required, are available by mail-order. The order form, with instructions on how to send off for any of the kits featured in this book, is on page 127.

The essence of this book lies in the designs themselves. They cover a wide range of subjects and styles and our choice over the years has been described as eclectic. They are based on medieval tapestry panels, Elizabethan embroideries, Indian painted manuscripts, oriental carpets, English country house chintzes, Islamic and Chinese porcelain and much else besides. The one unifying feature which gives such a disparate collection some sense of cohesion is the use of colour appropriate to tapestry. We have always eschewed gaudy or crude colouring. The slightly faded blending of tones found in all the most appealing old textiles can be seen in the designs in this book. I think this is true even of those designs which use strong or opalescent colours. The master of this technique is Kaffe Fassett, whose own needlepoint book promises to be a visual delight.

Nine years ago there was a real dearth of unusual or attractive tapestries to make. New colours and patterns that were seen in wallpapers, fabrics and interior decoration generally were not reflected in needlepoint. Since then things have changed beyond all recognition, and we are now able to produce designs that would have seemed far too adventurous when we started. The credit for this goes to the designers themselves and to a public that were, quite rightly, not prepared to put up with yet more of the same.

In selecting the designs for this book, from the accumulation of nine years' work, it has not been easy to know what to leave out. I hope that you will find a sufficiently wide range from which to pick at least one or two that you will enjoy working and keeping.

As with so many other subjects, there are certain terms in needlepoint where American and British usage differs. Since this is no technical tome, I have not given a 'translation' for every variable in the book, so I hope that American needleworkers will understand that for drawing pins they should read thumb tacks and cushions are what they would call pillows; and that English readers will not miss the description 'tapestry', a word which has not travelled across the Atlantic. Where there is a real risk of misunderstanding I have, of course, explained what is meant.

Measurements are given in both imperial and metric. These are not always exact equivalents, so to avoid any odd results, please follow one system or the other.

INTRODUCTION

As crafts go, embroidery on canvas is relatively young, dating back only to the sixteenth century. It developed from counted thread work, a type of embroidery in which geometrical stitches are worked on evenweave fabric, and which flourishes today in several forms including cross stitch. No one knows who first conceived the idea of covering the ground fabric entirely with stitching, but by the late 1500s this form of embroidery had become extremely fashionable.

At first canvas embroidery was valued mainly for its ability to imitate two more costly textile arts: woven tapestry (from which we doubtless get the popular name for canvas work, 'tapestry') and carpets, then used to cover tables. Using fine tent stitch, a skilled embroiderer could achieve with a needle the intricate detail and subtle shading created on vast looms at Les Gobelins, Beauvais and elsewhere. The rich pile of Turkish carpets could be duplicated with velvet stitch.

Producing these stitched tapestries and rugs became an important occupation for the mistress and staff of every large household. At relatively low cost – apart from the countless hours of work – bed hangings, wall hangings, upholstery and other furnishings could be provided, and many a spacious, but dark and draughty room made more inviting.

At times canvas work has been partially eclipsed by other forms of embroidery; at other times, as in the Victorian era, it has suffered a decline in the quality of its design. But its inherent usefulness and the relaxing nature of the work itself have ensured its survival even during such stagnant periods.

Today canvas embroidery is as popular as ever, and design, in this field as in all the applied arts, has undergone a quite dramatic transformation in recent years. Imaginative artists are re-interpreting traditional motifs and creating exciting new designs, exploiting the great variety of canvaswork stitches and even inventing new stitches for unusual effect.

In this book you will find a rich collection created by leading designers. Along with the chart and instructions for each design are suggestions for varying the design – by substituting a different stitch, perhaps, or abstracting and enlarging a single motif. We hope that some of these suggestions will inspire you to develop your own ideas. But even if you prefer to work the original designs as presented, you will have the satisfaction of creating something beautiful and distinctive.

MATERIALS

Canvas work need require only very basic materials: you can begin with no more than the canvas itself, thread in all the colours of the design, and a suitable needle.

Canvas

Originally the canvas used for this work was made of hemp; in fact, the word 'canvas' is derived from the Greek word for hemp, *kannabis*. Later it was made of linen. Today, the best canvas that is readily available is made of cotton; and in some countries you can find extra-fine canvas made of silk threads. Cheaper synthetic canvas is also available; and there is also a moulded plastic mesh, for small items such as coasters and boxes.

Conventional woven canvas is available in two main types: single thread, or mono, and double thread, or Penelope. Single thread is the more commonly used; it is suitable for any stitch and easy to work on because of the clarity of the mesh. Ordinary single canvas has a simple over-and-under weave, which has a tendency to become distorted through handling. This can be prevented to a great extent by using a frame, and it can also be corrected during the blocking process. Some stitches, such as basketweave, tent and cross stitch, distort the canvas less than others, such as slanted Gobelin.

A special kind of mono canvas, called interlock, is more stable. Its lengthwise threads are really double threads twisted tightly together; they hold the cross threads firmly, reducing distortion.

In double thread canvas, pairs of threads are woven together to produce an extra-firm fabric. This firmer construction permits you to jump from one part of the design to another; where the areas of stitching meet the joins will be imperceptible. By pushing the double threads apart gently with the needle, you can work areas of fine detail with four times as many stitches as when working over the double threads.

Canvas comes in a wide range of sizes, or gauges. These have not yet been metricated: 14-gauge and 16-gauge, for example, refer to canvas having 14 and 16 holes (or threads) per inch. For cushions, belts and chair seats the most frequently used gauges are between 10 and 14; for smaller items, such as evening bags, 16- or 18-gauge is suitable. For rugs, a double-thread rug canvas with 7 or even 5 holes per inch is normally used.

Canvas comes in a variety of colours, pastel shades, especially beige, being the most common. As even with the most careful stitching minute amounts of canvas will show through, choose a shade suitable for the colours in the design.

An alternative idea is to paint your design on the canvas (see Tracing the design on to canvas, page 10). This will not only mask any show-through of canvas, but will make the design easier to follow when stitching.

Always buy good-quality canvas. Avoid any that has knots or thin spots; it may damage the embroidery threads and will not wear well.

Threads

The threads most often used are made of pure wool and are spun specially for embroidery, being less stretchy than knitting yarns.

Tapestry (or tapisserie) wool is a smooth, four-ply yarn. It is always used in a single strand and is suitable for medium gauge (10-14 holes) canvas. Some brands are slightly thicker than others.

Crewel wool is a thin, two-ply yarn generally used with two or more strands in the needle. Being soft and fine (yet strong), it blends smoothly. Two colours can be used in the needle for subtle shading.

Persian wool is another two-ply yarn, somewhat thicker than crewel. It comes in a triple strand, which can easily be separated to give one or two strands as required.

For a glossy effect cotton threads can be used. A single strand of no. 3 perle cotton works well on 16-gauge, or no. 5 on 18-gauge. A small amount of a cotton thread can provide an attractive accent in an area stitched mainly in wool.

Needles

A tapestry needle has a blunt end which slips easily through the canvas mesh without snagging. Needles come in a wide range of sizes; the higher the number, the finer the needle. For 10- to 14-gauge canvas, a size 18 needle is most suitable.

Frames

It is quite possible to do good work without a frame, provided you stitch with an even tension. However, certain stitches will distort the work, no matter how skilled the embroiderer. A frame will help to keep the canvas threads properly aligned, and reduce the correction required by blocking. It will also prevent your over-handling the work and so keep it cleaner.

An embroidery ring frame cannot be used, as the canvas is too thick to fit between the two rings, but a stretcher frame – the kind used in oil paintings – is perfectly suitable. The stretchers, strips of moulding with mitred corners, are available from art supply shops and come in many different lengths. Buy two each of the required length and width of your canvas and assemble the frame by slotting the corner edges together. Remember that the design must fit within the *inner* edges of the frame, so buy the stretchers according to the measurement on the inner edge.

Mounting a canvas on a stretcher frame is shown on page 10.

A more sophisticated frame, the slate frame, is more expensive but can accommodate various sizes of canvas. Some fit on to a floor stand.

Other equipment

You will also need two pairs of scissors: large decorating shears for cutting the canvas and small embroidery scissors for cutting threads. Tweezers are useful for removing mistakes. You may also want a needle-threader and a thimble. Equipment and materials required for transferring the design, blocking and making up are specified under the relevant headings.

TRANSFERRING THE DESIGN

If you have purchased a tapestry kit, the design will normally have been printed on to the canvas in colours matching or nearly matching the threads to be used. All you have to do is the stitching.

Designs given in books and magazines may be in the form of a chart or in the form of a drawing or painting to be traced on to the canvas.

Following a chart

There are basically two kinds of chart used for canvas work designs: box charts and line charts. A line chart is, in a sense, the more realistic of the two. On this kind of chart the grid lines represent the actual canvas threads, so that each intersection of lines stands for one mesh. This type of chart is generally used where several different stitches are combined in one design.

On a box-chart (the kind used in this book) each square represents one canvas mesh or intersection. If the entire design is to be worked in half-cross or tent stitch (see page 12), it is easier to think of the squares as representing individual stitches. As on a line chart, the thread colours can be indicated either by symbols or by actual colours.

A design given in chart form can easily be varied in scale by choosing a larger- or smaller-gauge canvas. Suppose, for example, that your chart is 225 squares across and that you would like the work to measure about 18in across. Divide 225 by 18 to give you the number of stitches per inch. The result is 12.5, so the closest size is 12-gauge canvas. Check the finished size by dividing the number of squares on the chart by the canvas gauge: 225÷12=18¾in. The next size down, 14-gauge canvas, would give a measurement of 16in.

(When measuring in centimetres, you will need to multiply your number of stitches per centimetre by 2.5, as canvases are manufactured in mesh strands per inch.)

Copying a design

You may find a design that has to be traced on to the canvas. If it needs to be enlarged first, it will usually be printed with a grid superimposed on it. The degree of the enlargement will be indicated by a scale, such as 'Each square equals 5cm (2in)'. All you have to do is draw a grid containing the same number of squares as the grid covering the design, but making the squares the appropriate size.

Now copy the design freehand, using the lines of the grid as guides to positioning the various parts of the design.

Enlarging a design

You can easily enlarge any motif or drawing from another source. First trace the design from the original and draw a grid to cover your tracing. The more complex the design, the smaller the squares should be, as the more guidance you will need when reproducing it.

If the grid is square, draw a square of the desired size on a sheet of paper. Divide it into the same number of squares as the tracing and copy the design as described above.

If the design is not square, you will need to ensure that the proportions of the design are maintained. Tape the tracing with its overlaid grid near the lower left-hand corner of a large sheet of paper.

Draw two lines along the lower edge and up the left-hand side of the tracing, extending them a little beyond the intended finished size of the design. Measure off and mark the finished width or height on the base line.

Draw a diagonal line from the lower left through the upper right corner of the tracing, extending it slightly beyond the marked measurement. Draw a perpendicular line from the mark on the base line to the diagonal. From the point where these two lines meet, draw in the fourth side to meet the left-hand edge at a 90-degree angle. This completes the enlarged rectangle. Remove the tracing and, if you wish, erase the diagonal line. Construct the new grid and copy the design as described above.

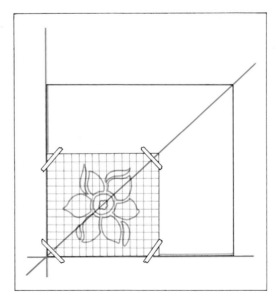

Go over the outlines with a black felt-tip pen so that they will be visible through the canvas, then colour in the design and, if necessary, indicate which stitches you plan to use.

An eye-catching collection of needlepoint cushions which includes designs from the Royal School of Needlework, Embroiderers' Guild, Susan Duckworth, Susan Skeen and the Victoria and Albert Museum.

Tracing the design on to canvas

Tape the canvas to the design, or hold it in place with weights. With a waterproof pen specially made for marking canvas (available from needlework shops), trace the four edges of the design, running the pen along the groove between two canvas threads. Then trace the design itself. Follow any curved or diagonal lines freely; don't attempt to follow the grid of the canvas.

Allow the ink to dry thoroughly for several hours before beginning to stitch.

If you like, you can paint the colours on to the canvas, as is done for most kits. Do not use watercolours, as these will run during the blocking process; even acrylics sometimes run, so avoid these, too. Use oil paints in a few basic colours (the art shop assistant can advise you), and mix these to get the required shades. Add a little turpentine and mix well. Test the consistency on some spare canvas: the colour should be bright and the paint just thin enough so that it doesn't clog the canvas mesh. The paint may take two or three days to dry.

PREPARING THE CANVAS

Cut the canvas 4-5cm (2in) larger all round than the size of the finished work. Bind the edges with masking tape to prevent them from unravelling, or machine stitch lengths of seam binding over the edges. The procedure is different if you are using a slate frame – see below.

Place the canvas on a piece of sturdy paper, such as blotting paper, and draw round the edges with a pencil. Keep this outline for use later when blocking the completed canvas.

If you are working from a chart, mark the vertical and horizontal centres of the canvas. The chart's centre should be marked with a cross. If this cross lies between stitches, mark the canvas between two threads either with a waterproof canvas-marking pen or with tacking. If the centre of the chart runs along a line of stitches, run the pen straight along a canvas thread at the vertical and horizontal centres. Begin stitching at the centre point of the design.

MOUNTING THE CANVAS ON A STRETCHER FRAME

Once the design has been transferred, or the centre marked, the canvas may be mounted on a frame.

Unless you are going to be undertaking a great deal of canvas work of different sizes, a stretcher frame is perfectly suitable. You will need to buy four stretchers, two each of the required length and width for your canvas (see Frames, page 6).

To mount your prepared canvas, first mark the centre point on each side of the frame, and on each side of the canvas. Match the centre mark of the top edge of the canvas to the corresponding mark on the frame, and fix it in place with drawing pins.

Working outwards to the edges, fasten the top edge of the canvas to the frame, placing the pins about 2cm (¾in) apart. Repeat along the bottom edge, pulling the canvas taut.

When fastening the side edges, begin by fixing the centre points as before, then work on one side then the other, from the centre to the edges, placing each tack opposite the other in tandem. This way you will be able to pull the canvas as taut as you can while distorting the weave as little as possible.

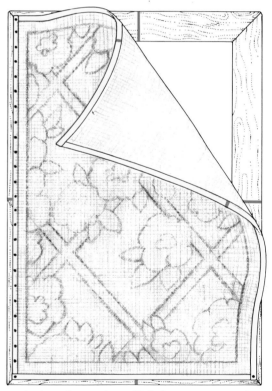

A slate frame is a slightly more complex piece of equipment but it has the advantage of being adjustable, which means it is suitable for canvases of varying sizes. Instead of being attached directly to the frame, the canvas edges are bound with webbing and then laced to the frame, which will have pegs or screws for adjusting the dimensions and ensuring a good taut canvas to work on. There are various types available and all come with instructions.

TO BLOCK A PIECE OF CANVAS WORK

When all the stitching is complete, the piece of embroidery must first be blocked, or stretched, before it is made up into the finished article. Even if it has been worked on a frame and is not distorted, it will look fresher after blocking; and if it has been pulled out of shape, blocking is essential.

You will need a piece of plywood or hardboard at least 5cm (2in) larger all round than the work, a hammer, carpet tacks, and the piece of blotting paper on which you have previously drawn the outline of the canvas. (If you have neglected to do this, draw a rectangle using two adjacent sides of the canvas as a guide to the measurements.)

Hold the work up to a strong light to make sure that no stitches are missing. Trim the thread ends closely on the wrong side. Clip the selvedge, if any, at short intervals; do not remove the masking tape.

Tape the blotting paper to the board and place the embroidery, wrong side up, on the board (first moistening it slightly if it is badly distorted). Tack it to the drawn outline at each corner. Continue tacking along all four sides, inserting the tacks at intervals of about 2cm (¾in).

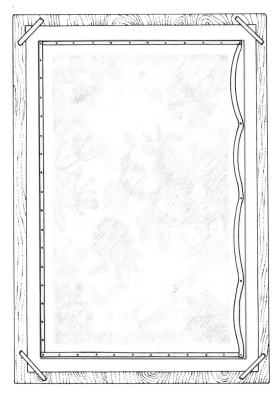

Dampen the work thoroughly, using either a sponge or a spray bottle. For most types of work you should now leave it to dry thoroughly – this may take several days for something as large and thick as a rug. But in certain circumstances the canvas should be removed from the board while still damp, in which case instructions for this will be given under the individual design.

BASIC STITCHING TECHNIQUES

To start work, make a knot in the thread and take the needle from the right side to the wrong side, a short distance ahead of the starting point. Do a few running stitches back to the starting point, then work over them in the stitch you have chosen. Stitch until you reach the knot, which you can then cut off. To end work, take the needle through the underside of a few stitches, then cut off the tail end of the yarn. A new thread can also be fastened by taking it through the wrong side of the stitches.

Canvas embroidery can be worked with either a 'sewing' or a 'stabbing' movement – unless, of course, the work is framed, in which case the stabbing movement must be used.

If you are left-handed, you may wish to reverse the direction of working shown in some of these diagrams. Many of the stitches, however, involve working in both directions. If you use the stabbing technique, you should be able to work comfortably in any direction; otherwise you will need to rotate the work in order to sew from right to left where necessary. So long as the stitches are correctly formed, it does not usually matter in which direction the work progresses.

Avoid using too long a thread. About 50cm (20in) is the recommended maximum length of thread for a small-scale stitch, such as tent, which entails many movements of the yarn. If the yarn becomes untwisted or kinks up, allow the needle to hang freely, and the yarn will resume its natural twist.

As a general rule, avoid bringing the needle up through a hole already partially filled with yarn. The needle will tend to split the strands, producing an untidy effect. Working down into the hole smooths the fibres and makes the stitches more clearly defined. In some of the more complex stitches, such as rice stitch, page 64, this rule must occasionally be broken, but where there is a choice, always come up into the hole containing the fewest threads.

STITCHES

There are many canvas-work stitches, producing many different textures. Some of the most effective and versatile, however, are the simplest ones.

To judge the effect of various stitches and combinations of stitches, it is useful to work some samples on a spare piece of canvas. This can then be kept as a reference when you wish to experiment. The gauge of the canvas and the type of yarn you choose will also vary the finished effect. Perle cotton, for instance, will add an attractive sheen.

The basic canvas-work stitch is called tent stitch. (It is also sometimes called petit point, but tent stitch is the term generally used by professional embroiderers.) The designs in this book are charted to be worked in either half-cross or tent stitch. Many canvas-work stitches are too angular, too highly textured, or both, to work well with these patterned designs. However, some will substitute happily for tent or half-cross and can be used effectively to emphasize an important part of the design, or to give textural interest to a background. Among the most useful are cross stitch and the Gobelin stitches.

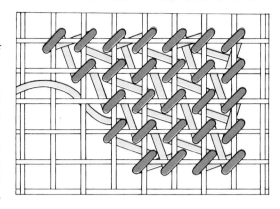

Tent stitch (basketweave)

This version of tent stitch is worked diagonally. It has two main advantages over continental stitch: it hardly distorts the canvas at all, and rows are worked back and forth, without having to turn the canvas or fasten off the thread. It is slightly less economical with thread.

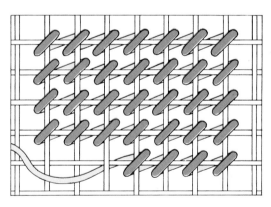

Tent stitch (continental)

This stitch, which covers one mesh of the canvas, may be worked either horizontally or vertically. It is best to fasten off the thread at the end of a row, or take it through to the underside of the work, and work all rows in the same direction, rather than rotating the canvas on alternate rows, which would entail bringing up the needle through a previously-worked stitch. Because this stitch tends to distort the canvas, it should be worked on a frame.

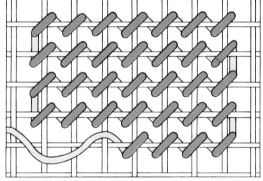

Half-cross stitch

This stitch appears virtually identical to tent stitch on the right side, but on the wrong side covers only the horizontal thread of the canvas. This makes it more economical on yarn but less firm. It is worked in rows, either horizontally or vertically. Take care not to pull the yarn too tightly. Half-cross should preferably be worked on either interlock or double thread canvas. If worked on ordinary single canvas, the stitches may slip under the vertical canvas threads. Half-cross can be worked back and forth as shown; because the work is less dense than continental tent, the previously worked stitch is less likely to be disturbed.

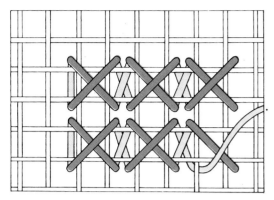

Cross stitch

Work this stitch either horizontally or vertically over two canvas threads (i.e. four meshes). For best results, work each row in two stages, completing the first 'leg' of each stitch, then going back over the work to complete the stitches. This will ensure that all the lower and all the upper parts of the stitch slant in the same direction, and it also helps to maintain an even tension. Cross stitch could be used to give a more textured effect to any design in this book. Choose a relatively fine canvas and work one stitch for each square on the chart. This stitch will, of course, enlarge the final design.

Encroaching Gobelin

This produces a smoother effect than upright Gobelin, because the ends of the stitches blend into each other. Each row is worked over at least three horizontal threads, two of which it shares with adjacent rows. Make sure always to take the needle down on the same side of the corresponding stitch of the row above.

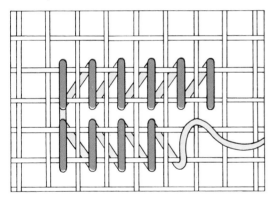

Upright Gobelin

The Gobelin stitches are named after the famous tapestry works in Paris, possibly because upright Gobelin resembles the ridged weave of tapestry. This stitch can be worked over two horizontal threads as shown, or it can be worked over three or more. A relatively thick thread should be used for longer stitches to prevent the vertical canvas threads from showing.

Slanted Gobelin is similar but, as the name indicates, is worked on a slight diagonal – normally over one vertical and two or more horizontal canvas threads. Unless worked on a frame, it distorts the canvas. It can also be worked with an 'encroaching' technique to blend the rows.

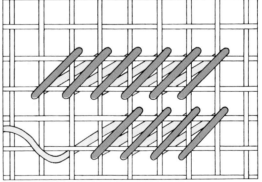

Wide Gobelin

This may also be considered a variation of continental tent stitch, since it is worked in the same way but over two meshes. It can be used effectively to add interesting texture to a large area of tent stitch in one colour – for example, in a background. Scattered short rows of wide Gobelin produce a slubbed effect similar to shantung.

Under the individual designs you will find suggestions and instructions for many other stitches. These can often be substituted for the basic stitch in all or part of the canvas, to give more textural interest or to create an unusual effect. Experiment.

A study in pastel from some of today's best designers: cushions by Kaffe Fassett, Susan Duckworth, Susanna Lisle, Susan Skeen and the Victoria and Albert Museum.

Making up a simple cushion cover

The inner cushion used should be the same size as the cover, or perhaps a little larger; this will ensure a good, plump fit, especially at the corners, which tend to wrinkle if a smaller pad is used.

The simplest way of making up a cushion is to place the embroidery and the backing fabric together with right sides facing, and stitch around three sides and part of the fourth, leaving a gap just large enough for inserting the pad. Then turn the cover right side out, insert the pad, and slipstitch the canvas edges together.

Inserting a zip

If you wish the cover to be removable, you can insert a zip in the backing fabric.

Cut two pieces of backing fabric, making each piece the height of the finished cover and half the width, plus 2cm (¾in) seam allowance on all edges.

Pin the two pieces together (with right sides facing) along one vertical edge. Stitch at either end, taking a 2cm (¾in) seam allowance and leaving a gap 2cm (¾in) longer than the zip; then tack with small stitches (or the longest machine stitch) along the zip opening. Press the seam open.

Turn under and press 5mm (¼in) on the seam allowance of one piece. Place this along the edge of the zip as shown, with the slider 1.5cm (½in) below the top of the tacking, the pull tab extended, and all the fabric lying to the right. Pin and tack through the fold of fabric and the zip.

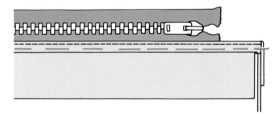

Stitch by machine, using a zipper foot, or by hand, using a small, spaced backstitch, close to the edge of the fold.

Place the fabric right side up and opened out, with the zip lying flat underneath and with the pull tab turned down. Pin and tack along the remaining edges of the zip, through all layers. Stitch by hand using backstitch, or by machine. Remove all tacking, including the stitches holding the opening together.

When making up the cover, open the zip first and stitch around all four edges. Turn the cover right side out through the zip opening then insert the inner cushion.

To make up a round cushion

It is more satisfactory to make a cover for a 'box' cushion, since a 'knife-edge' cover, although it looks easier to construct, usually puckers round the edge.

Buy the cushion first and measure it: you will need enough fabric for the underside of the cover plus a strip (cut on the straight) to form the gusset, usually 5cm (2in) by the circumference of the cushion, plus enough bias strips to make up piping for both edges. (Remember to add on seam allowances.) You will also need piping cord and a zip (optional).

Trim the canvas to within 2cm (¾in) of the work. Use this piece to cut a circle from the fabric. (If using a zip, cut two semi-circles, adapting the method described left.)

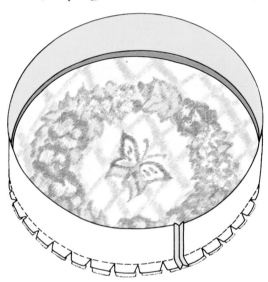

Cut the gusset strip to the required measurements, and join the short ends to form a ring. Make up two lengths of piping. Insert the zip in the backing piece, if required.

Tack the piping to the edge of the embroidered circle, joining the ends as described on page 48. Tack the other length of piping to the edge of the fabric circle.

Place the gusset on the embroidered circle, right sides facing, and edges matching, enclosing the piping; tack it in place. Using the zipper foot (or working by hand with backstitch) stitch the gusset to the canvas, working close to the piping cord. Notch the edges of the seam allowances.

Join the remaining edge of the gusset to the fabric circle in the same way. If a zip has been used, leave it open and stitch all the way around; if not, leave one-third of the seam unstitched. Insert the pad and hand-stitch the gap closed.

ROYAL SCHOOL OF NEEDLEWORK

The Royal School of Needlework was founded in 1872 by Princess Christian, daughter of Queen Victoria, with the object of 'restoring ornamental needlework to the high place it once held among the decorative arts'.

Much outstanding embroidery has been carried out by the School's workrooms including the Coronation Robes worn by Queen Elizabeth the Queen Mother in 1937 and by Queen Elizabeth II at her coronation in 1953. Specially commissioned work is constantly carried out in all fields of embroidery. The Overlord panel, for example, is the biggest work of its kind in the world.

The workroom conserves and restores antique embroidery and tapestries, cleans and repairs lace and samplers, mounts finished works, while the Design department interprets customers' requirements into individual designs, both traditional and modern. These include Coats of Arms, large panels, chair seats, slippers, etc.

The School has day, evening and short courses in all types of embroidery, as well as an apprenticeship scheme. We can only include a few designs from the Royal School of Needlework, but the School's shop stocks a vast range of kits, books, frames, threads including pure silks, golds and linens, canvases, linen fabrics and accessories.

Royal School of Needlework
25 Princes Gate
London SW7 1QE
Telephone: 01 589 0077

Victorian Bird and Paradise Bird

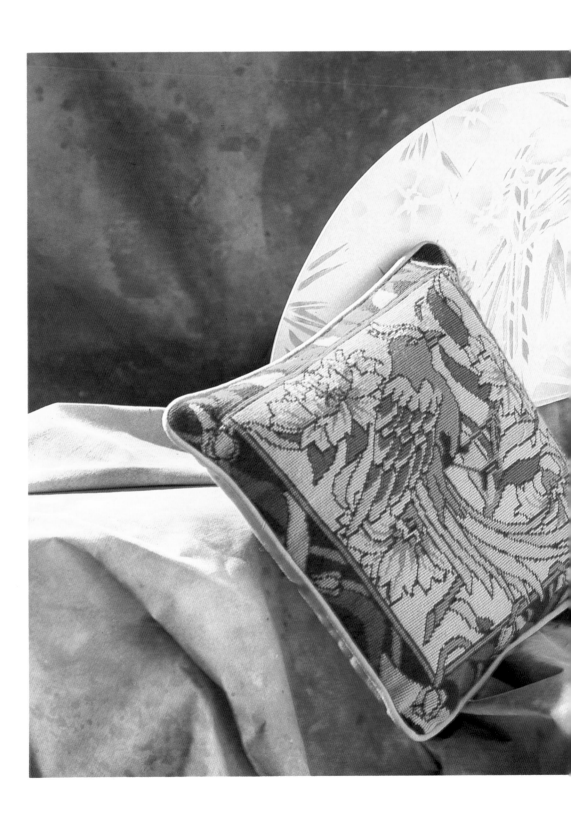

Ehrman have always included in their range some designs from the Royal School of Needlework's famous collection. They are chosen from a huge selection in the School's design department, which includes several dating from the nineteenth century, when William Morris, Walter Crane and Edward Burne Jones were all connected with the School.

Victorian Bird was designed in 1980 by Susan Skeen and loosely based on the work of William Morris.

Victorian Bird (left) *proved immensely popular when it appeared in 1980 and so was followed two years later by Paradise Bird. They make a charming pair of cushions, linked by their shared colours blue, yellow, russet and green.*

William Morris modestly described himself as 'an ornamentalist, a maker of would-be pretty things'. He is, in fact, rightly regarded as one of the greatest textile designers ever and his obituary notice in the *Daily Chronicle* of 5 October 1896 emphasized the scope of his activities: 'Whatever he touched he gave life to and, like Michelangelo, Blake, Rossetti, he chose more than one medium for giving shape to the things of the charmed world in which he lived. And with Morris the decorative art comes first. His poetry, or a great part of it, exists for exactly the same purpose as his tapestries, flowered linens, silken embroideries – to express the beauty of colour, line and material.'

Morris began by designing embroideries for his own home, the Red House, in about 1860 and his earliest embroideries were seen as substitutes for tapestries. His first tapestry, 'The Vine and Acanthus', the only one he wove with his own hands, was used later for one of the most popular embroidery designs issued by the Morris firm. (Amateur needlewomen were able to buy designs and materials from the firm of Morris, Marshall, Faulkner and Co., and in many ways he can be seen as the first designer and producer of canvas work or embroidery kits. A fine example to emulate!)

The popularity of Morris designs spawned a host of imitators and greatly influenced firms like Liberty of Regent Street which had started in 1875.

Although flowers and trees were a primary source of inspiration, William Morris used all forms of nature in his designs and birds are a familiar feature. It has to be said, however, that he favoured the more common species such as thrushes, woodpeckers and doves – a bird of paradise and our hybrid 'Victorian bird' would have been rather too exotic for him!

Variations
If you prefer, you could work the border in flat stitch (page 115), using blue and green and alternating them in chequerboard style. Or use the same colours in rice stitch (page 64). If you are using Persian or crewel wool, you could mix the colours in the needle and work the border in half-cross or tent stitch. (The inner edge of the border will need to be straightened if a square stitch, such as flat or rice, is used.)

The design could also be adapted for use as a panel. Use 16-gauge canvas and work it in perle cotton for a glossy finish.

Materials

Tapestry wool (see colourways). The amounts given are calculated for half-cross stitch. To work the design in basketweave or continental tent, increase all amounts by 50 per cent. If either of these stitches is used, an ordinary mono canvas may be substituted for double thread or interlock. Two strands of Persian wool or three strands of crewel can be substituted for the single strand of tapestry wool used for this design.

12-gauge double or mono interlock canvas, 45cm (18in) square
Size 18 tapestry needles
40cm (16in) furnishing fabric for backing
1.5m (5ft) narrow piping cord
Cushion 35cm (14in) or 38cm (15in) square
30cm (12in) zip fastener (optional)
Slate or stretcher frame (optional)
Tools and materials for preparing canvas (see page 10) and for blocking (page 11).

The finished cushion measures 35cm (14in) square.

Working the embroidery

Prepare the canvas and mount it on the frame, if used (see page 10). Following the chart on the right, work the design in half-cross stitch (or basketweave or continental tent stitch).

Blocking and making up

Block the completed work (see page 11) and allow it to dry thoroughly. Trim the canvas edges, leaving margins of 2cm (¾in).

From the backing fabric cut a piece 39cm (15½in) square. Or, if inserting a zip, cut two pieces as specified on page 16.

From the remaining fabric, cut and join bias strips to cover the piping cord (see page 48). Make up the piping.

Insert the zip, if desired, in the back cover.

Attach the piping to the back cover as described on page 48.

Join the front and back covers as described on page 16, and insert the cushion.

COLOURWAYS FOR VICTORIAN BIRD

Ap934 (PA321)	*a*	
Ap403 (PA612)	*b*	
Ap205 (PA863)	*c*	
Ap353 (PA644)	*d*	
Ap562 (PA585)	*e*	
Ap141 (PA491)	*f*	
Ap331 (PA745)	*g*	

Ap = Appleton
PA = Paterna

Yarn amounts

a	117m	(129yd)
b	59m	(65yd)
c	59m	(65yd)
d	59m	(65yd)
e	15m	(17yd)
f	59m	(65yd)
g	59m	(65yd)

**COLOURWAYS
FOR PARADISE
BIRD**

Ap934 (PA321) *a*

Ap562 (PA585) *b*

Ap403 (PA612) *c*

Ap353 (PA644) *d*

Ap205 (PA863) *e*

Ap141 (PA491) *f*

Ap331 (PA745) *g*

Ap = Appleton
PA = Paterna

Yarn amounts
a	117m	(129yd)
b	59m	(65yd)
c	40m	(44yd)
d	31m	(34yd)
e	31m	(34yd)
f	10m	(11yd)
g	25m	(28yd)

Materials
Tapestry wool (see colourways). The amounts given are calculated for half-cross stitch. To work the design in basketweave or continental tent, increase all amounts by 50 per cent. If either of these stitches is used, an ordinary mono canvas may be substituted for double thread or interlock. Two strands of Persian wool or three strands of crewel can be substituted for the single strand of tapestry wool used for this design.

12-gauge double or mono interlock canvas
    45cm (18in) square
Size 18 tapestry needle
40cm (16in) furnishing fabric for backing
1.5m (5ft) narrow piping cord
Cushion 35cm (14in) or 38cm (15in)
    square
30cm (12in) zip fastener (optional)
Slate or stretcher frame (optional)
Tools and materials for preparing canvas
    (see page 10) and for blocking

The finished cushion measures 35cm (14in) square.

Working the embroidery
Prepare the canvas and mount it on the frame, if used (see page 10). Following the chart on the left, work the design in half-cross stitch (or basketweave or continental tent stitch).

Blocking and making up
Block the completed work (see page 11) and allow it to dry thoroughly. Trim the canvas edges, leaving the standard margins of 2cm (¾in).

From the backing fabric cut a piece 39cm (15½in) square. Or, if inserting a zip, cut two pieces as specified on page 16.

From the remaining fabric, cut and join bias strips to cover the piping cord (see page 48). Make up the piping.

Insert the zip, if desired, in the back cover.

Attach the piping to the back cover as described on page 48.

Join the front and back covers as described on page 16, and insert the cushion.

Honeysuckle Chair Seats

This classic design, shown in two different colourways, can be adapted for virtually any chair seat simply by adjusting the dimensions of the background area.

The central garland is inspired by the floral designs of the Art Needlework Movement of the 1880s. Simple and decorative, their designs were a reaction against the loud tones of the popular style of Berlin Woolwork. The aim in these designs was to achieve the effect of canvas work after two hundred years of fading, rather than reproduce the vibrant colours of the seventeenth-century originals. The Movement's designs were the first to use a range of soft colours and the results look remarkably contemporary a century later.

The chair seats shown here have been worked with dark green and powder blue backgrounds, but you could substitute another colour, if you wish – for example, wine red, dark brown, navy blue or black.

The honeysuckle design would be equally well suited to a cushion, or a footstool. First establish the finished size you would like, then adjust the design if necessary. Do not make the background too large; the flowers should fill most of the area. If you need to enlarge the design, you might choose a finer canvas and work in cross stitch (page 13). Calculate the gauge of canvas required as instructed on page 6.

Materials
Tapestry wool (see colourways). The amounts given are calculated for half-cross stitch. To work the design in basketweave or continental tent, increase all amounts by 50 per cent. If either of these stitches is used, an ordinary mono canvas may be substituted for double thread or interlock. Two strands of Persian wool or three strands of crewel can be substituted for the single strand of tapestry wool used for this design.
12-gauge double or mono interlock canvas
   65cm (26in) square, (or to fit chair seat,
   plus 5cm (2in) all round)
Size 18 tapestry needle
Chair with removable seat pad
Slate or stretcher frame (optional)
Tools and materials for preparing canvas
   (see page 10) and for blocking.

The motif measures approximately 32cm (12½in) in diameter; the yarn amounts for the background are for a seat measuring 50cm (20in) each way.

Working the embroidery
Remove the chair seat and measure it carefully, taking the tape measure over the rounded surface down to the lower edges. Measure from front to back and along the front and back edges. Draw the outline of the embroidered area on the canvas, using a canvas marking pen. Decide on the positioning of the motif, and mark the centre point of the motif on the canvas. Mark the vertical centre of the canvas, the horizontal centre of the motif and the horizontal centre of the canvas (which will probably be slightly above the centre of the motif). Bind the edges of the canvas and mount the work on the frame, if used (see page 10).

Following the chart overleaf, work the design in half-cross stitch (or basketweave or continental tent stitch).

Blocking and making up
Before blocking the work, make sure that the embroidered area completely covers the pad of the chair. If it does not, add a few rows of stitches around the edges.

Block the work and remove it from the board while it is still slightly damp. Mark the centre point of each side.

Do not trim away the canvas.

In addition to the chair you will need some drawing pins, upholstery tacks and a hammer; a piece of cotton sateen curtain lining makes a neat finish for the underside of the work.

Remove the pad or seat from the chair. Measure and mark the centre point on each side. Place the embroidery right side down on a flat surface and lay the pad, upside down, on top. Using the drawing pins, fasten the work to the underside of the pad, close to the edge, beginning by fastening the centre points. On a rectangular or trapezoidal shape, continue by fastening the four corners. Then insert drawing pins along all sides, placing them about 2cm (¾in) apart and checking frequently to make sure the work is taut and straight. Adjust pins as required.

This is a versatile and simple chair seat cover that goes well with almost any type of chair. We chose a dusty blue and a sharper bottle green for the backgrounds, but many other colours could be used instead.

COLOURWAYS FOR HONEYSUCKLE CHAIR SEATS

Ap694 (PA703)   *a*

Ap696 (PA700)   *b*

Ap692 (PA754)   *c*

Ap403 (PA612)   *d*

Ap401 (PA613)   *e*

Ap223 (PA932)   *f*

Ap222 (PA933)   *g*

Ap221 (PA490)   *b*

The blue background colour shown on page 25 is Ap324 (PA512). The green background colour shown on page 25 is Ap406 (PA600). You will need 190m (209yd).

Ap = Appleton
PA = Paterna

Yarn amounts
a	16m	(18yd)
b	14m	(16yd)
c	21m	(23yd)
d	27m	(30yd)
e	30m	(33yd)
f	10m	(11yd)
g	25m	(28yd)
b	30m	(33yd)

When you are sure the work is smooth and taut, fasten it permanently with the upholstery tacks, removing the drawing pins as you go. Trim away the excess canvas.

To neaten the underside of the work (optional), cut a piece of curtain fabric slightly larger than the underside of the pad. Turn under and press the edges, then slipstitch them to the edges of the canvas.

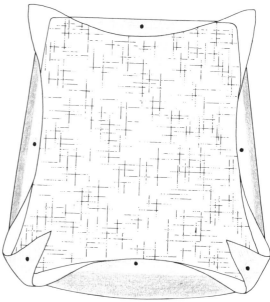

The method of making up a footstool or round chair seat is the same, but with a circular shape you will need to place the pins slightly closer together and make small pleats in the canvas to gather in the fullness.

Floral Footstool and Trellis and Butterfly Footstool

It takes a special skill to translate flowers on to canvas. A painter has an infinite palette of colours with which to capture all the different tints of a rose's petal, but in needlepoint it may only be practical to incorporate perhaps four or five colours when stitching an entire bloom.

The pretty wreath of flowers which features on the Floral Footstool is made up of a very traditional summer bouquet: honeysuckle, simple briar roses, morning glory and ivy entwined on a dark chocolate background. Yet, despite its intricacy, the whole design uses only eleven different shades of yarn. Flowers always pose problems for the needlework designer but the

morning glory was a particular challenge. Instead of darkening towards the centre, like most flowers, its delicate trumpets fade almost to white, making it extremely difficult to convey a sense of depth and a natural shape.

Trellis and Butterfly was designed by Virginia Crowe for a popular women's magazine. It has a lovely summery feel to it, the old-fashioned flowers – including roses, violets and pansies – which make a circlet round the butterfly are a reminder of country gardens. The pale trelliswork in the background helps to link the two and also subtly provides an extra dimension to the final design.

Floral Footstool is an adaptation of a Victorian pattern from the Royal School of Needlework's own archives. As well as making a charming small cushion, the design could be adapted to make a fine chair seat cover.

Opposite page: Old-fashioned cottage-garden flowers combine well with the butterfly and the background trellis. Its delicate colouring would make this a very pretty round cushion for a bedroom.

**COLOURWAYS
FOR FLORAL
FOOTSTOOL**

Ap992 (PA263) *a*

Ap947 (PA941) *b*

Ap754 (PD281) *c*

Ap401 (PA613) *d*

Ap645 (PA662) *e*

Ap545 (PA611) *f*

Ap744 (PA561) *g*

Ap601 (PA324) *h*

Ap471 (PA727) *i*

Ap241 (PD531) *j*

Ap584 (PD115) *k*

Ap = Appleton
PA or PD = Paterna

Yarn amounts

a	12m	(13yd)
b	10m	(11yd)
c	13m	(14yd)
d	21m	(23yd)
e	12m	(13yd)
f	15m	(17yd)
g	13m	(14yd)
h	12m	(13yd)
i	19m	(21yd)
j	15m	(17yd)
k	88m	(97yd)

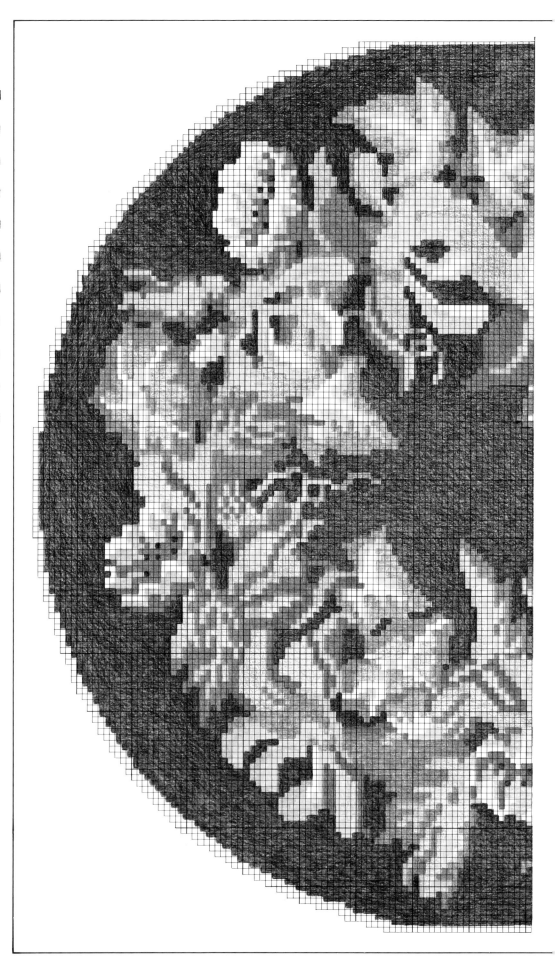

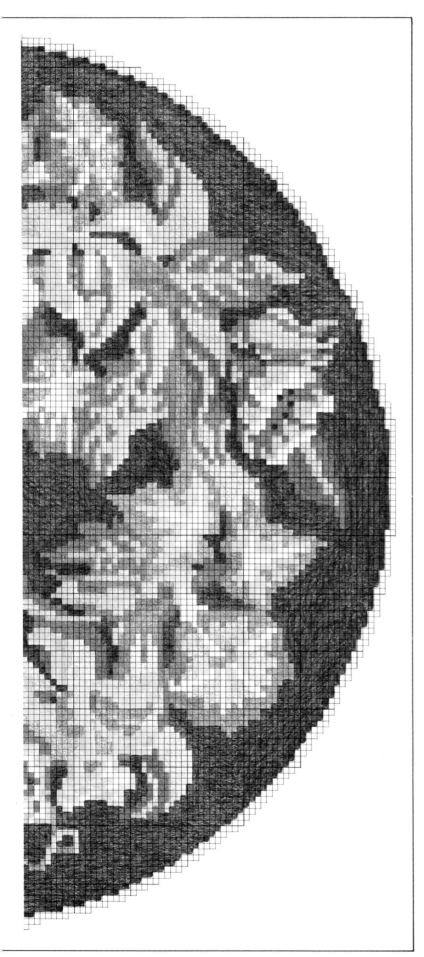

Materials

Tapestry wool (see colourways). The amounts given are calculated for half-cross stitch. To work the design in basketweave or continental tent, increase all amounts by 50 per cent. If either of these stitches is used, an ordinary mono canvas may be substituted for double thread or interlock. Two strands of Persian wool or three strands of crewel can be substituted for the single strand of tapestry wool used for this design.

14-gauge double or mono interlock canvas 40cm (16in) square

Size 20 tapestry needle

Footstool with pad, 25cm (10in) in diameter

Slate or stretcher frame (optional)

Tools and materials for preparing canvas (see page 10) and for blocking (page 11).

Working the embroidery

Prepare the canvas and mount it on the frame, if used (see page 10). Following the chart on the left, work the design in half-cross stitch (or basketweave or continental tent stitch).

Blocking and making up

Block the completed work (see page 11). Remove it from the board while it is still slightly damp. Do not trim the canvas edges.

Mount the work on the footstool pad as described on pages 24-7.

Variations

This design is equally well suited to a round cushion. Choose the cushion pad first; it should be a 'box' type, rather than a 'knife edge', and the same size or slightly larger than the finished embroidery. Follow the instructions for making up a round cushion given on page 16.

The design could also be used for a chair seat cover. Measure the chair pad carefully, and draw the outline of the area to be embroidered on the canvas. Mark the centre of the design and also mark the vertical centre of the canvas. In most cases – chair seats generally being slightly trapezoid in shape – it will be best to position the design a few canvas threads to the front of the horizontal centre; mark this point on the vertical centre, and centre the design in relation to this point. Follow the instructions for mounting a chair seat given on pages 24-7.

Like Trellis and Butterfly Footstool, there are many helpful flower ideas here.

Materials

Tapestry wool (see colourways). The amounts given are calculated for half-cross stitch. To work the design in basketweave or continental tent, increase all amounts by 50 per cent. If either of these stitches is used, an ordinary mono canvas may be substituted for double thread or interlock. Two strands of Persian wool or three strands of crewel can be substituted for the single strand of tapestry wool used for this design.

14-gauge double or mono interlock canvas
    40cm (16in) square
Size 20 tapestry needle
Footstool with pad, 25cm (10in) in
    diameter
Slate or stretcher frame (optional)
Tools and materials for preparing canvas
    (see page 10) and for blocking (page 11).

Working the embroidery

Prepare the canvas and mount it on the frame, if used (see page 10). Following the chart on the right, work the design in half-cross stitch (or basketweave or continental tent stitch).

Blocking and making up

Block the completed work (see page 11). Remove it from the board while it is still slightly damp. Do not trim the canvas edges.

Mount the work on the footstool pad as described on pages 24-7.

Variations

Any of the floral motifs in the ring could be used on its own for a bookmark. Reduce the motif's size by using 18-gauge canvas. Place the motif towards one end of the area to be worked, which should be about 20×5cm (8×2in). Use two strands of crewel wool or one of Persian or perle cotton.

Butterflies are charming subjects for embroidery and can be adapted and used in all sorts of ways. Make a tracing of the butterfly (outline only) from the chart and enlarge it slightly (see page 7). Make another tracing the same size as the original, so that you have one small and one larger butterfly. Arrange these on a piece of paper to make a pleasing design. Colour them as you like.

COLOURWAYS FOR TRELLIS AND BUTTERFLY FOOTSTOOL

Ap756 (PA903) *a*

Ap703 (PA694) *b*

Ap354 (PA603) *c*

Ap406 (PA600) *d*

Ap961 (PA464) *e*

Ap992 (PA263) *f*

Ap943 (PA955) *g*

Ap462 (PA544) *h*

Ap843 (PA703) *i*

Ap552 (PA772) *j*

Ap749 (PA500) *k*

Ap606 (PA311) *l*

Ap451 (PA323) *m*

Ap = Appleton
PA = Paterna

Yarn amounts
a   4m   (5yd)
b   16m (18yd)
c   8m   (9yd)
d   12m (13yd)
e   14m (16yd)
f   36m (40yd)
g   6m   (7yd)
h   7m   (8yd)
i   1m   (1yd)
j   2m   (2yd)
k   8m   (9yd)
l   5m   (6yd)
m   4m   (5yd)

Chippendale Rose

A typical mid-eighteenth century composition. The seventeenth century in England was best known for embroidered pictures and samplers, but with the turn of the century there was a return to objects meant for practical use. Canvas work became very popular and was used for making chair seats, cushion covers and large wallhangings. Bold flowers along with hunting scenes were the most popular emblems. They were arranged in bunches, vases, garlands and festoons and were boldly drawn in bright, naturalistic colours on plain backgrounds. Chippendale Rose is a perfect example of this style and red was a popular background colour for such cushion covers.

Similar designs with large flowers and leaves were popular for embroidered carpets which came back into favour at this time. They were worked in tent stitch and must have taken many months to complete. Their curling, naturalistic, leaf patterns acted as inspiration for William Morris 150 years later. Contemporary books of flower engravings, often intended to help embroiderers, were useful sources of design and, towards the middle of the century, embroidery patterns began to appear in publications such as the *Lady's Magazine* of the early 1760s, foreshadowing the flood of printed designs which were to appear in the following century.

Variations
Almost any of the flower motifs in this design could be adapted and used on its own. The central rose is especially suitable. Trace it from the chart and enlarge it, if you like (see page 7). If you wish to work it (enlarged) in one of the basic stitches, such as half-cross, you will need to add more colours to give it depth and interest. Plan your design on paper using coloured pencils, then refer to this plan while working the embroidery.

Another approach is to work the rose in a textured stitch. Flat stitch (page 115) or rice stitch (page 64) would be suitable. Cross stitch (page 13) could be used for the centre. Work samples of the stitches using the chosen yarns to see the effect before you begin working the design.

Materials
Tapestry wool (see colourways). The amounts given are calculated for half-cross stitch. To work the design in basketweave or continental tent, increase all amounts by 50 per cent. If either of these stitches is used, an ordinary mono canvas may be substituted for double thread or interlock. Two strands of Persian wool or three strands of crewel can be substituted for the single strand of tapestry wool used for this design.

12-gauge double or mono interlock canvas, 45cm wide by 40cm deep (18×16in)
Size 18 or 19 tapestry needle
40cm (16in) furnishing fabric for backing
1.5m (5ft) narrow piping cord
Cushion 37×32cm (14½×12½in) (if this size is not available, make your own following the instructions on page 79)
25cm (10in) zip fastener (optional)
Slate or stretcher frame (optional)
Tools and materials for preparing canvas (see page 10) and for blocking (page 11).

The finished cushion measures approximately 35cm (14in) wide and 30cm (12in) deep, excluding piping.

Working the embroidery
Prepare the canvas and mount it on the frame, if used (see page 10). Following the chart overleaf, work the design in half-cross stitch (or basketweave or continental tent stitch).

Blocking and making up
Block the completed work (see page 11) and allow it to dry thoroughly. Trim the canvas edges, leaving margins of 2cm (¾in).

From the backing fabric cut a piece 39cm (15½in) wide and 34cm (13½in) deep. From the remaining fabric, cut and join bias strips to cover the piping cord (see page 48). Or, if inserting a zip, cut two pieces as instructed on page 16.

Insert the zip, if using, in the back of the cover (see page 16).

Attach the piping to the back cover as described on page 48, then join the front and back covers as described on page 16.

Chippendale Rose is a perfect example of mid-eighteenth century style, when red was a popular background for such cushion covers. It would go particularly well with any wooden furniture.

**COLOURWAYS
FOR
CHIPPENDALE
ROSE**

Ap991b (PA260) *a*

Ap584 (PA421) *b*

Ap504 (PA840) *c*

Ap528 (PD500) *d*

Ap502 (PA841) *e*

Ap154 (PA534) *f*

Ap403 (PA612) *g*

Ap764 (PA435) *h*

Ap252 (PA653) *i*

Ap695 (PA701) *j*

Ap562 (PA585) *k*

Ap843 (PA703) *l*

Ap = Appleton
PA or PD = Paterna

Yarn amounts

a	50m	(55yd)
b	33m	(37yd)
c	21m	(23yd)
d	10m	(11yd)
e	62m	(68yd)
f	10m	(11yd)
g	17m	(19yd)
h	3m	(4yd)
i	10m	(11yd)
j	22m	(24yd)
k	10m	(11yd)
l	14m	(16yd)

Stitch Variations

If you would like to add some textural interest to this design, you might work the petals and foliage in kelim stitch. This simple stitch resembles knitting and can be worked in either vertical or horizontal rows. Work the rows so that they slant in alternating directions, as shown.

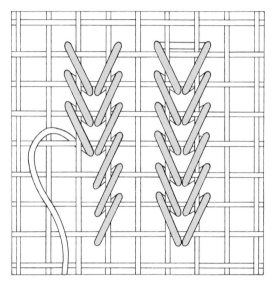

Before beginning to stitch, plan the direction of the stitching for each leaf and petal. Make a rough tracing of the design and mark the directions on it.

To retain some of the shading of the original, use crewel or Persian wool so that you can mix colours in the needle. For example, the blue flower in the lower right-hand corner might be worked with mid-blue and light blue yarns mixed at the base of each petal and light blue alone towards the ends.

Work the flower centres in cross stitch (page 13), the background in tent stitch and the border in encroaching upright Gobelin.

For the veins of leaves and other lines, work stem stitch on top of the finished canvaswork. To work stem stitch:

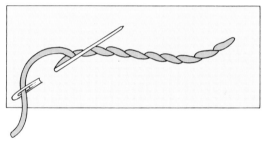

SUSAN DUCKWORTH

Susan Duckworth is one of the country's leading knitwear designers and these two cushions are her first, and very successful, needlepoint designs. It is not surprising that she should have decided to do them as she originally trained as a painter and her interests have always included Elizabethan blackwork, Victorian samplers and the patterning of oriental carpets. These influences are seen very clearly in her knitwear.

'Having spent some fifteen years concentrating on designing knitted garments, I found it a very exciting challenge to translate my knitting designs into tapestry patterns. The approach to tapestry is a refreshing change after the fairly time-consuming task of working on hand-knitted swatches. All that is required for a tapestry is a painting which is transferred on to canvas and then cleverly stitched by an experienced needlewoman.'

After a spell at the make-up department of the BBC, she joined the 401½ studios in London. In the early 1970s, under the guidance of its founder, Michael Haynes, this was a meeting place for many of the outstanding designers and craftsmen of the time. At first she produced one-off designs, but by 1973 she had her own thriving workshop with one hundred outworkers and a year's contract as a knitwear designer for Gudule in Paris. She now shows her collections annually in Milan, New York and London and is also a member of the London Designer Collections.

Oakleaves and Acorns

The original cushion on which this design is based is a deep, faded red and that could act as a good basis for colour variations. It was worked by Bess of Hardwick, one of history's most famous needlewomen.

With Mary Queen of Scots she em-broidered the Oxburgh Hangings in 1570 which are now in the Victoria and Albert Museum. These panels depict animals, birds, fish and fabulous creatures. Hard-wick Hall, built by Bess between 1591 and 1597, is perhaps the most splendid and least

The oak-leaf pattern of this design has been used by Susan Duckworth in her knitwear and can be adapted in all sorts of ways. An excellent example of effective non-naturalistic colours.

altered of all Elizabethan houses. It now belongs to the National Trust and houses the magnificent collections of tapestry and needlework panels accumulated by her. It also houses her own embroidery works and those she did with Mary Queen of Scots. Often a noble household would include a professional embroiderer to direct the work, even though the bulk of it may be done by the mistress of the house, and we know that Bess of Hardwick had her maids and even the grooms and boys of the household stitching away.

Bess of Hardwick was one of the most colourful characters of her age. Born in 1520, the daughter of a Derbyshire squire of fairly modest means, she proceeded to make a succession of four marriages becoming richer and more powerful with each. Through her second husband, Sir William Cavendish, she inherited Chatsworth and when her fourth husband, the immensely wealthy Earl of Shrewsbury died, she set about building her colossal new house, Hardwick Hall, at the age of seventy. The Long Gallery, 166 feet long and decorated with thirteen Flemish tapestries and many family portraits is one of the great rooms of England.

While using Bess of Hardwick's cushion for inspiration, Susan Duckworth has created a design that is clearly her own, with its distinctive colouring and modern spirit.

Variations

The particular colour combination shown here might be called a 'bedroomy' one, which combines well with modern pastel decorations. But it is easily adapted to other colourways. The first time this design appeared – on a sweater – it had a red background and a lot of bright emerald green in the leaves. You could go either for a naturalistic or a stylized effect; try terracotta as a background with shades of browns, cream and greens in the leaves. Plan your colour scheme with coloured pencils on a tracing of the chart.

The oakleaves would look good worked on a chair seat and matching chairback (ideal for a William and Mary oak chair), adapting the pattern to suit the style of chair. The instructions for covering a chair seat are given on pages 24-7.

As this design began life as a sweater, you might like to adapt the motif to something you could wear: a pillbox hat and matching clutch bag would be an interesting use of the motif and simple to make up.

The oakleaves could also be used for a handsome bell pull. You might work the leaves in flat stitch (page 115) worked over 3 canvas threads, using kelim stitch (page 38) for the background. If you use crewel or Persian wool for the work, you could mix two shades of yarn in the needle to give the leaves a rich depth of colour.

Materials

Tapestry wool (see colourways). The amounts given are calculated for half-cross stitch. To work the design in basketweave or continental tent, increase all amounts by 50 per cent. If either of these stitches is used, an ordinary mono canvas may be substituted for double thread or interlock. Two strands of Persian wool or three strands of crewel can be substituted for the single strand of tapestry wool used for this design.

12-gauge double or mono interlock canvas
　　50×40cm (20×16in)
Size 18 tapestry needle
40cm (16in) furnishing fabric for backing
1.6m (5½ft) narrow piping cord
Cushion 40×30cm (16×12in)
25cm (10in) zip fastener (optional)
Slate or stretcher frame (optional)
Tools and materials for preparing canvas
　　(see page 10) and for blocking.

The finished cushion measures 40×30cm (16×12in).

Working the embroidery

Prepare the canvas and mount it on the frame, if used (see page 10). Following the chart overleaf, work the design in half-cross stitch (or basketweave or continental tent stitch).

Blocking and making up

Block the completed work (see page 11) and allow it to dry thoroughly. Trim the canvas edges, leaving margins of 2cm (¾in).

From the backing fabric cut a piece 34cm deep by 44cm wide (13½×17½in). Or, if inserting a zip, cut two pieces as specified on page 16.

From the remaining fabric, cut and join bias strips to cover the piping cord (see page 48). Make up the piping.

Insert the zip, if using, in the back cover.

Attach the piping to the back cover as described on page 48.

Join the front and back covers as described on page 16, and insert the cushion.

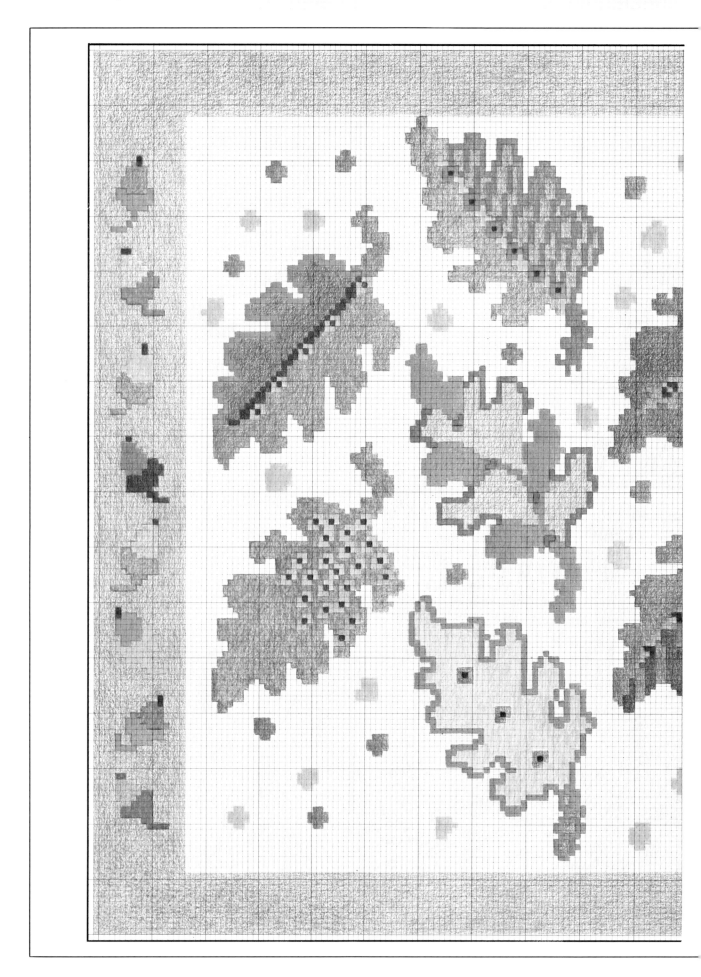

COLOURWAYS FOR OAKLEAVES AND ACORNS

Ap124 (PA483) *a*

Ap603 (PA313) *b*

Ap711 (PA914) *c*

Ap755 (PD234) *d*

Ap311 (PA733) *e*

Ap851 (PA755) *f*

Ap155 (PA532) *g*

Ap743 (PA563) *b*

Ap877 (PA948) *i*

Ap606 (PA321) *j*

Ap153 (PA534) *k*

Ap = Appleton
PA or PD = Paterna

Yarn amounts
a   42m   (46yd)
b   11m   (12yd)
c   10m   (11yd)
d   10m   (11yd)
e   3m   (3yd)
f   10m   (11yd)
g   5m   (6yd)
b   8m   (9yd)
i   70m   (77yd)
j   4m   (5yd)
k   8m   (9yd)

Urns and Fruit

These urns were inspired by the enchanting paintings Susan Duckworth found in the old Shaker ABC book. 'Once you are struck by a theme you begin to see it everywhere,' she says, and she finds herself experimenting with a new-found motif in numerous different ways. This cushion is based on one of Susan Duckworth's knitwear designs and was originally done in fine cotton yarn with much complicated stitching. On canvas, of course, the finer stitches enable you to incorporate more detail and to reproduce a more curved, fluid line, well suited to working in needlepoint.

The Shaker ABC or 'abecedarius' is a whimsical world of animals created for the practical purpose of teaching reading. Richard Barsman introducing the book says: 'The Shakers behaved soberly, but they were not dull, and the stern codes that regulated their communal life in matters of worship, dress and eating did not restrict the human spirit . . . At home and in school Shaker children learned about barnyard animals, but with this delightful alphabet they could also roam with the mythical Xanthos, the Ichneumon, and the Basilisk. Their education may have been simple, but evidently it was fun as well.'

The Shakers believed in self-sufficiency and equality in all things. Founded in 1774, in Hancock, Massachusetts, their high point was in the 1850s. But after this a decline set in; growth from within was impossible as the Shakers banned marriage and sexual relations. In 1850 they numbered 6000 but the last male shaker died in 1960 and now only a handful of elderly women remain.

Mauves and purples are not colours usually associated with needlework and it is very refreshing to see them used so skilfully by Susan Duckworth. She trained originally as a painter and it can always be seen in her masterly mix of colours.

Variations

This design can be varied and adapted in many ways. You could choose a different colour for the background, for instance, but it should be dark to provide adequate contrast with the motifs.

You could give the cushion a stitched sampler look by working each urn in a different stitch, using flat stitch (page 115), rice (page 64), cross (page 13), and weaving stitch, shown here. Work the background in encroaching slanted Gobelin (page 13) or in continental tent, with short scattered lines of wide Gobelin (page 13). Work the flowers and butterfly in continental tent, adding French knots (page 90) and stem stitch (page 38) to emphasize details.

To work weaving stitch:

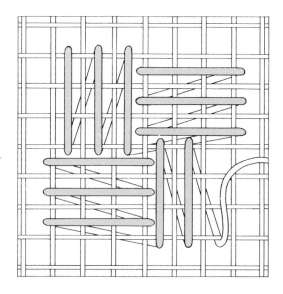

Another possibility is to use only one of the urn motifs and enlarge it to fill the whole area (re-positioning the butterflies as you like). You could work the motif in cross stitch on 16-gauge canvas, which would enlarge it by one-half. You could then add an abstract border using a mixture of colours and/or stitches to make it the size you would like.

For a splendid array of harmonizing cushions, make four as described above, using a different motif for each cushion.

To make a flat cushion

Many of the designs in this book can be adapted to make a flat cushion for a chair. In addition to the materials for the embroidery, you will need fabric for backing (as for a loose or scatter cushion), piping cord, and a piece of plastic foam about 3cm (a good inch) thick and slightly smaller all round than the cushion cover.

Before working the embroidery, measure the chair seat. Depending upon its

shape, you may want to make a paper pattern so that the cushion will fit the seat fairly accurately. Draw the outline of the embroidery on the canvas. You may need to add a plain border or adjust the design in some other ways to suit the area of the particular seat.

When the work is completed and blocked to shape, cut a piece of backing fabric the same size, plus seam allowances. Make up the piping, if desired. From the remaining fabric cut two strips (or four, if the cushion will be attached to all four legs), making them 4cm wide and about 40-45cm long (1½×16-18in). Fold each strip lengthways, right sides facing, and stitch across one end and along the side, 1cm (½in) from the edge. Trim the seam allowances slightly and turn the tie right side out. Press; turn in and slipstitch the raw edges at the open end.

Make up the cushions as for the simple cushion cover described on page 16, inserting piping, if used, and leaving an opening at the back for inserting the foam pad. Slipstitch the opening. Hand stitch the centre of each tie to the cushion, just under the seam.

These rich colours go remarkably well with pale fabrics, as the pastel blues and pinks of the photograph illustrate.

**COLOURWAYS
FOR URNS AND
FRUIT**

Ap106 (PA320) *a*

Ap101 (PA313) *b*

Ap324 (PA512) *c*

Ap153 (PA514) *d*

Ap694 (PA734) *e*

Ap121 (PA924) *f*

Ap451 (PA322) *g*

Ap503 (PA951) *h*

Ap752 (PA946) *i*

Ap741 (PA563) *j*

Ap222 (PA873) *k*

Ap = Appleton
PA = Paterna

Yarn amounts

a	115m	(127yd)
b	35m	(39yd)
c	6m	(7yd)
d	8m	(9yd)
e	8m	(9yd)
f	6m	(7yd)
g	9m	(10yd)
h	8m	(9yd)
i	11m	(12yd)
j	16m	(18yd)
k	9m	(10yd)

Materials

Tapestry wool (see colourways). The amounts given are calculated for half-cross stitch. To work the design in basketweave or continental tent, increase all amounts by 50 per cent. If either of these stitches is used, an ordinary mono canvas may be substituted for double thread or interlock. Two strands of Persian wool or three strands of crewel can be substituted for the single strand of tapestry wool used for this design.

12-gauge double or mono interlock canvas 50cm (20in) square
Size 18 tapestry needle
50cm (20in) furnishing fabric for backing
1.8m (6ft) narrow piping cord
Cushion 38cm (15½in) or 40cm (16in) square
35cm (14in) zip fastener (optional)
Slate or stretcher frame (optional)
Tools and materials for preparing canvas (see page 10) and for blocking (page 11).

The finished cushion measures 38cm (15½in) square.

Working the embroidery

Prepare the canvas and mount it on the frame, if used (see page 10). Following the chart on the left, work the design in half-cross stitch (or basketweave or continental tent stitch).

Blocking and making up

Block the completed work (see page 11) and allow it to dry thoroughly. Trim the canvas edges, leaving margins of 2cm (¾in).

From the backing fabric cut a piece 42cm (17in) square. Or, if inserting a zip, cut two pieces as specified on page 16.

From the remaining fabric, cut the join bias strips to cover the piping cord (see page 48). Make up the piping.

If adding a zip, insert in the back cover.

Attach the piping to the back cover as described on page 48.

Join the front and back covers as described on page 16, and insert the cushion.

Piping

A piped edge gives a cushion a professional-looking finish and is well worth the small amount of extra work.

Buy enough piping cord to go around the edges of the cushions, plus a little extra for joining. The fabric used is normally the same as that used for the back of the cushions. Avoid very thick fabrics and those that fray easily. For best results the strips should be cut on the bias (at a 45-degree angle to the selvedge).

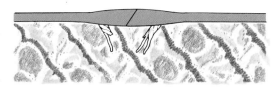

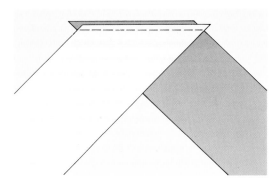

Cut strips of fabric, making the width equal to the circumference of the piping cord plus twice the seam allowance. Join strips, if necessary, on the straight grain, as shown.

Wrap the strip around the cord, right side outside, and machine stitch close to the cord, using a zip foot.

Pin and tack the piping to the back of the cushion cover, placing the cord inside the seamline, so that the seam allowances lie towards the edge. Clip the piping seam allowances at the corners to make them lie flat.

If the piping is narrow, the ends may simply be overlapped. If the piping is thick, end the tacking about 5cm (2in) to either side of the chosen joining point and unpick the stitching for the same distance. Join the fabric ends on the straight grain as described above; trim and press the seam. Cut the cord so that the ends overlap by 2-3cm (about 1in). Cut away two strands from one end and one from the other (see above); wind the remaining strands together and bind them with thread. Fold the fabric over the cord and tack it in place.

Stitch the piping in place, just outside the seamline.

Tack the back of the cover over the front, right sides facing, enclosing the piping. Stitch it in place, using the zipper foot, working as close as possible to the cord. Leave a gap for turning, unless a zip has been inserted in the back.

SUSANNA LISLE

'I became interested in tapestry design through being involved with Ehrman, first exhibiting watercolours in their gallery, then illustrating the covers of their tapestry catalogues when they first came out. I am primarily a painter and trained for two years at Leeds, then in Fine Art at Goldsmiths School of Art. My work has always been traditional and figurative and the sources of inspiration for my tapestry designs have been the same as for my painting and illustrative work: flowers, landscapes, people and the combination of these with furniture and interiors. With tapestry I enjoy seeing the effects that are produced through turning flat paint into a stitched surface. The charm is in the way the stitches add a quirky but sensitive quality to the drawn form. Drawing is the most important ingredient and the basis for all my work; I work hardest at this aspect on any design. In this area I have been much influenced by my father, who taught David Hockney drawing at Bradford, and favourite artists such as Degas, Bonnard and Matisse. I love the care they take with drawing and colour and also their choices of subject matter. Added to this is my mother's influence from the world of costume and textiles on which she lectures. This has made me appreciate embroidery, tapestry and knitting as works of art in themselves. Designing for tapestry combines all these elements and there is the challenge of interpreting someone's ideas for a specific project.'

Chintz

Based on eighteenth-century English chintz patterns, this design is a typically florid one featuring full-blown roses and honeysuckle climbing over a trellis. Modern chintz patterns, popularized by companies like Colefax and Fowler, are often reworkings of these earlier patterns which in turn developed from imported Indian chintzes. It was in the sixteenth century, with the spread of middle-class wealth, that the demand for decorative household fabrics started and the brightly coloured, exotic

fabrics of India were highly prized in Europe.

From 1640 the East India Company was commissioning special designs for European taste and after 1680 the demand for all kinds of chintzes grew explosively. They were used as wallcoverings as well as for stools, cushions and beds, and by the mid-seventeenth century whole rooms were decorated in chintz. The best known of the late eighteenth century bed furnishings are those associated with the 'Garrick bed' in the Victoria and Albert Museum. These chintzes were sent from India in 1774 as a gift to the wife of the actor, David Garrick. Then in 1669 the English East India Company began sending actual patterns for the Indian cotton painters to copy and detailed measurements were supplied for the making-up of bed curtains with matching valances, bedspreads and quilts.

Later chintz designs became more European in flavour with rococo columns and floral bouquets influenced by European silk designs. Nowadays 'chintz' is used to describe any cotton or linen furnishing fabric of floral pattern stained with fast colours.

Variations

Any one or all three of the central rose motifs could be adapted to serve as the design for a smaller cushion – round or square – or for a round footstool. Trace the motifs from the chart, and enlarge them as described on page 7 so that they fill most of the area to be worked.

If you wish to follow the original design exactly, mark the centre of the area to be worked and the chosen centre of the rose motif(s) on the original chart. Then work the embroidery starting from the centre and moving outwards, following the chart. If you choose to work in this way, you will need to calculate in advance the gauge of canvas that will produce motifs of the size you want. A 10-gauge canvas will enlarge the motif by 20 per cent. For a greater increase, you will need to choose a finer canvas and work 4 stitches (or a single cross stitch) for every square on the stitch guide.

If you prefer, you can work the design more freely. In this case, trace the enlarged motif on to the canvas (see page 7). Then use the colours as you please.

This design could be used for a striking and unusual envelope handbag. Choose a 14-gauge canvas to reduce the size slightly, then add a border in a solid colour, about 3cm or 1in deep, to each end of the design. The finished measurements of the bag, when closed, will be approximately 30cm wide and 15cm deep (12×6in).

As with many designs in the book, chintz lends itself to different colourways. If you prefer the blue version in the picture on page 50, use the illustration overleaf as a colour guide and substitute the thread shades listed below.

Materials

Tapestry wool (see colourways). The amounts given are calculated for half-cross stitch. To work the design in basketweave or continental tent, increase all amounts by 50 per cent. If either of these stitches is used, an ordinary mono canvas may be substituted for double thread or interlock. Two strands of Persian wool or three strands of crewel can be substituted for the single strand of tapestry wool used for this design.

12-gauge double or mono interlock canvas
    55×45cm (22×18in)
Size 18 tapestry needle
40cm (16in) furnishing fabric for backing
1.8m (6ft) narrow piping cord
Cushion 35×45cm (14×18in)
30cm (12in) zip fastener (optional)
Slate or stretcher frame (optional)
Tools and materials for preparing canvas
    (see page 10) and for blocking (page 11).
The finished cushion measures 35×45cm (14×18in).

Working the embroidery

Prepare the canvas and mount it on the frame, if used (see page 10).

Following the chart overleaf, work the design in half-cross stitch (or basketweave or continental tent stitch).

Blocking and making up

Block the completed work (see page 11) and allow it to dry thoroughly. Trim the canvas edges, leaving margins of 2cm (¾in).

From the backing fabric cut a piece 39cm deep by 49cm wide (15½×19½in). Or, if inserting a zip, cut two pieces and attach zip as specified on page 16.

From the remaining fabric, cut and join bias strips to cover the piping cord (see page 48). Make up the piping. Attach the piping to the back cover as described on page 48.

Join the front and back covers as described on page 16, and insert the cushion.

Tradional chintzes, damasks, faded carpets and good quality furniture all epitomize the 'English Country House' look which is admired around the world and which never goes out of fashion. These cushions would look very much at home in a country house setting but it is nice to see them here in the garden which brings out their colours beautifully.

COLOURWAYS FOR PINK CHINTZ

Ap149 (PA900)   *a*

Ap151 (PA901)   *b*

Ap296 (PA600)   *c*

Ap544 (PA612)   *d*

Ap694 (PA703)   *e*

Ap742 (PA653)   *f*

Ap746 (PA560)   *g*

Ap942 (PA945)   *h*

Ap945 (PA943)   *i*

Ap946 (PA951)   *j*

Ap991 (PA260)   *k*

Ap = Appleton
PA = Paterna

Yarn amounts

a	10m	(11yd)
b	27m	(29yd)
c	24m	(27yd)
d	33m	(36yd)
e	24m	(27yd)
f	12m	(13yd)
g	7m	(8yd)
h	24m	(27yd)
i	17m	(18yd)
j	25m	(28yd)
k	62m	(68yd)

**COLOURWAYS
FOR BLUE
CHINTZ**

Ap749 (PA571)
   10m (11yd)
Ap744 (PA561)
   19m (21yd)
Ap824 (PA550)
   16m (18yd)
Ap461 (PA564)
   31m (34yd)
Ap431 (PA622)
   36m (40yd)
Ap293 (PA603)
   28m (31yd)
Ap842 (PA734)
   19m (21yd)
Ap861 (PA804)
   19m (21yd)
Ap863 (PA800)
   14m (16yd)
Ap962 (PA203)
   28m (31yd)
Ap877 (PA948)
   64m (71yd)

Ap = Appleton
PA = Paterna

EMBROIDERERS' GUILD

Embroiderers' Guild is an educational charity, founded in 1906 to promote the craft of embroidery to the highest possible standards. The patron of the Guild is HRH Princess Alice, The Duchess of Gloucester.

The Guild is housed in one-time Grace and Favour apartments at Hampton Court Palace where regular workshops and lectures on all aspects of embroidery are held and exhibitions of historical and contemporary embroidery are displayed. The apartment also houses a unique collection of historic and modern embroideries and a comprehensive library.

Membership of the Guild is open to anyone with an interest in embroidery. All full and associate members receive a newsletter, published in mid-February and mid-August and full members are entitled to use all the facilities of the Hampton Court apartments. Visits to places of historical interest, renowned for their embroideries, both at home and abroad, form a part of the regular programme arranged for members. *Embroidery*, the Guild's magazine, is published in March, June, September and December.

Apartment 41
Hampton Court Palace
East Molesey
Surrey KT8 9AU
Telephone: 01 943 1229

Fox and Crane

This scene from Aesop's fable 'The Fox and the Crane' is taken from an eighteenth-century embroidered purse in the Embroiderers' Guild collection at Hampton Court Palace.

Materials
Tapestry wool (see colourways). The amounts given are calculated for half-cross stitch. To work the design in basketweave or continental tent, increase all amounts by 50 per cent. If either of these stitches is used, an ordinary mono canvas may be substituted for double thread or interlock. Two strands of Persian wool or three strands of crewel can be substituted for the single strand of tapestry wool used for this design.
12-gauge double or mono interlock canvas, 55cm wide by 35cm deep (22×14in)
Size 18 tapestry needle
50cm (20in) furnishing fabric for backing
1.8m (6ft) narrow piping cord
Cushion, 45×35cm (18×14in)
30cm (12in) zip fastener (optional)
Slate or stretcher frame (optional)
Tools and materials for preparing canvas (see page 10) and for blocking (page 11).

The finished cushion measures 45×35cm (18×14in).

Working the embroidery
Prepare the canvas and mount it on the frame, if used (see page 10).
Following the chart overleaf, work the design in half-cross stitch (or basketweave or continental tent stitch).

Blocking and making up
Block the completed work (see page 11) and allow it to dry thoroughly. Trim the canvas edges, leaving margins of 2cm (¾in).
From the backing fabric cut a piece 49cm deep and 39cm wide (19½×15½in). Or, if inserting a zip, cut two pieces as specified on page 16. Also cut two strips, across the width of the fabric, each 10cm deep and 49cm wide (4×19½in).
From the remaining fabric, cut and join bias strips to cover the piping cord (see page 48). Make up the piping.

Insert the zip, if used, in the back cover.
Join the two strips to the long edges of the embroidery. Press the seams open.
Attach the piping to the back cover as described on page 48.
Join the front and back covers as described on page 16, and insert the cushion.

Variations

This stylized design would lend itself to alternative colour schemes. For example, you might work it in shades of grey – from silver to charcoal – on a deep red background, working the outlines in black. To make sure that your chosen colour scheme will work, trace the design from the chart, following the outlines roughly. Then fill in the design with coloured pencils as close as possible to your chosen yarn colours.

Reduced slightly in size, the design would make an attractive picture. Use a 16-gauge canvas; this will produce a picture approximately 34×14cm (13½×5½in). Use a single strand of perle cotton for the stitching.

This design could also be adapted to cross stitch worked on an evenweave fabric, with the background left unworked. Choose a beige or cream evenweave with 24 threads to 2.5cm (1in) and naturalistic colours (trying them on paper first, as described above). Add a decorative border. (Books containing borders can be found in libraries and art supply shops.)

This needlework is a long, thin panel, so we bordered it top and bottom only, to make it a suitable shape for a bolster cushion. It can often be useful to border two sides as this gives you flexibility with the shape of cushion you can use.

COLOURWAYS FOR FOX AND CRANE

Ap998 (PA221)	*a*
Ap963 (PA212)	*b*
Ap182 (PA473)	*c*
Ap962 (PA203)	*d*
Ap902 (PD531)	*e*
Ap241 (PA643)	*f*
Ap693 (PA734)	*g*
Ap647 (PA531)	*h*

Ap = Appleton
PA or PD = Paterna

Yarn amounts

a	43m	(48yd)
b	5m	(6yd)
c	9m	(10yd)
d	13m	(15yd)
e	13m	(15yd)
f	24m	(27yd)
g	20m	(22yd)
h	36m	(40yd)

Turkish Stripe

This splendid design, which is equally suitable for a cushion or a footstool top, was inspired by a beautiful piece of eighteenth-century Persian embroidery in the Embroiderers' Guild collection. The original design was on a fragment from a pair of wonderfully embroidered trousers of the type worn by Persian women at court.

With this design we have tried to reproduce the original colours as faithfully as possible and have simply enlarged the design to make a cushion cover.

Paintings of eighteenth- and nineteenth-century court life in Persia show women wearing tunics and straight-legged trousers, the silk covered with the most lavish embroidery in designs similar to this.

Materials

Tapestry wool (see colourways). The amounts given are calculated for half-cross stitch. To work the design in basketweave or continental tent, increase all amounts by 50 per cent. If either of these stitches is used, an ordinary mono canvas may be substituted for double thread or interlock. Two strands of Persian wool or three strands of crewel can be substituted for the single strand of tapestry wool used for this design.

14-gauge double or mono interlock canvas
  55cm wide by 50cm deep (22×20in)
Size 20 tapestry needle
50cm (20in) furnishing fabric for backing
Cushion, 45×35cm (18×14in)
1.8m (6ft) narrow piping cord
30cm (12in) zip fastener (optional)
Slate or stretcher frame (optional)
Tools and materials for preparing canvas
  (see page 10) and for blocking (page 11)

The finished cushion measures approximately 44×37cm (17½×14½in).

Working the embroidery

Prepare the canvas and mount it on the frame, if used (see page 10).

Following the chart overleaf, work the design in half-cross stitch (or basketweave or continental tent stitch).

Blocking and making up

Block the completed work (see page 11) and allow it to dry thoroughly. Trim the canvas edges, leaving margins 2cm (¾in).

From the backing fabric cut a piece 48×41cm (19×16½in). Or, if inserting a zip, cut two pieces as specified on page 16.

From the remaining fabric, cut and join bias strips to cover the piping cord (see page 48). Make up the piping.

If adding a zip, insert in the back cover.

Attach the piping to the back cover as described on page 48.

Join the front and back covers as described on page 16, and insert the cushion.

Variations

This canvas adapts easily to use on a footstool. Follow the instructions for mounting a chair seat or footstool top on pages 24-7.

The design could be used instead for a beautiful rug. If, for example, 7-gauge canvas were used instead of 14, the rug would measure approximately 88×74cm (35×29½in). See instructions for making up a rug on page 108. Sketch the stripes in a number of alternative ways to find the best combination.

You could also adapt the design for use on a piano bench. To plan the work you will need a piece of graph paper with as many spaces as the narrower side of the chart and some coloured pencils. Following the stitch guide, continue charting the design until your chart, combined with the original guide, is in the correct proportions for the bench seat.

COLOURWAYS FOR TURKISH STRIPE

Ap881 (PA261) *a*

Ap583 (PA421) *b*

Ap749 (PA500) *c*

Ap255 (PA651) *d*

Ap757 (PA902) *e*

Ap302 (PA484) *f*

Ap154 (PA534) *g*

Ap241 (PD531) *h*

Ap762 (PA436) *i*

Ap331 (PA745) *j*

Ap = Appleton
PA or PD = Paterna

Yarn amounts

a	59m	(65yd)
b	66m	(73yd)
c	117m	(129yd)
d	20m	(22yd)
e	88m	(97yd)
f	30m	(33yd)
g	30m	(33yd)
h	16m	(18yd)
i	15m	(17yd)
j	14m	(16yd)

Red House

The sampler pattern is reproduced here on fine 17-mesh canvas. It is stitched in crewel wool, unlike all the other designs in the book which are worked in tapestry wool.

Samplers are an endless source of inspiration and there are numerous embroidery patterns and kits available based on seventeenth and eighteenth century examples. This bright and cheerful one looks very much at home photographed here in the kitchen.

The original was signed by Richard Harrison, 1740, and was worked in cross stitch throughout. The design is also unconventional for that time, having a border of vertical bands in alternate colours of red and yellow covering almost a quarter of the depth and across the whole top of the sampler. The elegant, well-proportioned house, typical of the early 1700s, is red brick and is surrounded by a formal garden with fir trees and flowering trees beyond. The soft yellow canvas is left unstitched in the background areas.

Samplers are frequently referred to in Elizabethan and even earlier writings but there are few surviving examples from that period. In the seventeenth century girls received rigorous training in embroidery and samplers served as technical exercises. Pastoral scenes and country houses were popular themes for canvas and crewel work or for flat silk embroidery. Sampler making was very popular in the nineteenth century and there were printed instructions for them. They were far more technically proficient than the older ones with just their tent and cross stitch.

Samplers make very attractive pictures when they have the irregularity of the novice. The alphabet, often in conjunction with stylized flowers, animals and trees, is a common theme and it is easy to understand why they now command such high prices at auction. The Red House might inspire you to reproduce your own house or garden with a similar, effective simplicity.

Variations

The house can be used as it is and a different border substituted for the one shown here. For example, you might use a border of equal width instead of the proscenium border, using flat stitch (page 115) in two contrasting colours. Or work the border in rice stitch. This versatile stitch can be worked in either one or two colours. Its knobbly texture predominates if it is worked in one colour; if a contrasting colour is used for the corner stitches a lattice effect is produced.

To work rice stitch:

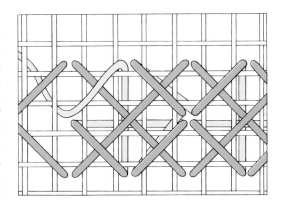

The design could also be worked in cross stitch on evenweave cotton or linen fabric. Choose an evenweave with 26 threads to 2.5cm (1in). The design will measure approximately 40cm deep by 44cm wide (16×17in), so you will need a piece of fabric at least 55cm wide (20×22in). Use a single strand of *coton à broder* or perle cotton for the embroidery, or three strands of stranded cotton. Work the cross stitch over two horizontal and two vertical threads, as when working on canvas.

Materials

Crewel wool (see colourways). The amounts given are calculated for half-cross stitch. To work the design in basketweave or continental tent, increase all amounts by 50 per cent. If either of these stitches is used, an ordinary mono canvas may be substituted for double thread or interlock. A single strand of Persian wool can be substituted for the two strands of crewel wool used for this design.

17-gauge mono interlock pale yellow or
    cream canvas, 40cm deep by 45cm wide
    (16×18in)
Size 22 tapestry needle
Sheet of stiff cardboard 30×32cm
    (12×12½in)

Strong thread for lacing
Slate or stretcher frame (optional)
Tools and materials for preparing canvas
  (see page 10) and for blocking (page 11).

The finished panel measures 30cm deep by 32cm wide (12×12½in).

Working the embroidery
Prepare the canvas and mount it on the frame, if used (see page 10).

  Following the chart overleaf, work the design in half-cross stitch (or basketweave or continental tent stitch), using two strands of crewel wool. The background is left unworked.

Blocking and making up
Block the completed work (see page 11) and allow it to dry thoroughly. Do not trim the canvas edges.

  Lace the work over the stiff cardboard as described on page 68. The tapestry can then be professionally framed.

Red House is based on a charming sampler from the Embroiderers' Guild collection. It is dated 1740 and the bold geometric design in fresh, cheerful colours is remarkable for the period.

COLOURWAYS FOR RED HOUSE

Ap866 (PA850) *a*

Ap948 (PA940) *b*

Ap844 (PA711) *c*

Ap471 (PA727) *d*

Ap463 (PA544) *e*

Ap464 (PA542) *f*

Ap242 (PA652) *g*

Ap296 (PA660) *h*

Ap621 (PA845) *i*

Ap712 (PA912) *j*

Ap992 (PA262) *k*

Ap = Appleton
PA = Paterna

Yarn amounts
a	86m	(95yd)
b	43m	(48yd)
c	69m	(76yd)
d	47m	(52yd)
e	18m	(19yd)
f	45m	(50yd)
g	29m	(32yd)
h	32m	(35yd)
i	47m	(52yd)
j	18m	(19yd)
k	53m	(59yd)

Mounting a panel or box lid

The method described here can be used for a panel (which should then be framed professionally) or for covering a piece of card to form a box lid. You will need a piece of thick card or hardboard slightly larger (if for a panel) than the finished work. If the margin is to fit under the rebate of a frame moulding, it is best to select the moulding and measure the depth of the rebate before cutting the board. If in doubt, make the margin scant, as an overlap is obviously preferable to a line of unworked canvas. You will also need some panel pins and strong thread.

Place the work right side down and lay the board on top of it. Fold down one long edge of the canvas and pin it to the edge of the board, leaving the required margin on the right side of the work. Repeat on the other long edge.

Thread a large needle with the strong thread, without cutting it from the reel. Starting at the centre, lace the two edges together as shown, working through them alternately. Fasten the thread at one end. Cut off a generous length from the reel, and work to the opposite end. Before fastening off, pull the stitches firmly along the whole length to make sure the work is taut, and check that the margins of unworked canvas are equal. Fasten off and remove the panel pins or thumb tacks.

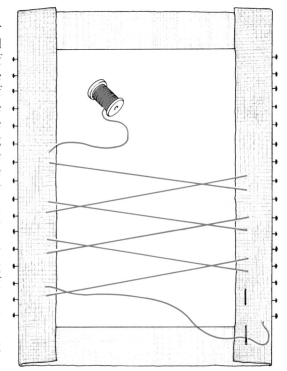

Repeat the lacing process on the remaining edges, folding the corners neatly.

If you are mounting a circular piece of needlework, lace from one side to the other, always across the widest part of the circle, working round in a sunburst pattern until the work is secure. Ripples of canvas between stitches should be cut away afterwards to reduce bulk.

SUSAN SKEEN

Susan Skeen is one of the most imaginative new needle-work designers to have emerged in the last few years. Like so many of the best designers she is not restricted to one particular field and has undertaken commissions from knitwear companies as well as having exhibitions of her drawings and embroideries in Oxford and London. She graduated with first class honours in textile design from Loughborough College of Art and Design and then went to work at the Royal School of Needlework from 1978 to 1982. Here she was involved in every aspect of design from the creative to the highly technical matching and adapting of traditional canvaswork. After a spell teaching at Dartford in London she joined *Homes and Gardens* in 1985 and is now their furnishing fabrics editor.

Her tapestries are usually full of bright and unusual colours and the flowers, shells, leaves and birds are meticulously detailed. They manage to be both impressive and cheerful at the same time and she will often give traditional subject matter a contemporary reinterpretation.

Three Birds

A very traditional type of nineteenth century design is given a totally different feel with a new set of colours. The birds and exotic foliage are inspired by lush Victorian panels and compositions associated with Berlin Woolwork. In the 1840s restraint was thrown to the winds and overblown flowers such as full roses or heavy, waxy lilies were depicted with clarity on dark backgrounds. Here, however, the feel of the colours, bold but light, is better suited to chintzes or primary coloured fabrics. The birds are particularly interesting being stitched in greys and white with only the smallest flecks of colour. It almost looks as if a colour television has gone wrong and portrayed them, alone on the cushion, in black and white! This adds to the three-dimensional quality of the picture.

Variations

The cushion might be enlarged slightly by adding a narrow fabric border, as described below. Alternatively, you could add an embroidered border, using either half-cross stitch, tent stitch, encroaching upright Gobelin (page 13), or rice stitch (page 64).

You could make a pair of pictures, using the left-hand and right-hand birds. Trace the birds from the chart, adjusting the outlines as necessary to make the birds complete. Work each bird on canvas measuring 30cm (12in) square.

OTHER IDEAS

Fabric borders

A fabric border is particularly effective with cushion designs that have a lot of pictorial interest at the edges, or an especially interesting stitched border, since it allows more of the design to be visible.

The first step in making a fabric border is to cut a pattern for the four strips. Decide on the finished size of the cover (which should be the same size, or slightly smaller than the cushion). Subtract the width/depth of the embroidery from this final size of the cover. Divide the result by 2; this gives the *finished* depth or width of the border.

For the pattern, cut a rectangular piece of paper with the long sides measuring the same as one side of the cover, plus seam allowances and the short sides the finished depth of the border plus seams.

To shape the pattern, fold it in half to mark the centre. With the strip still folded, measure along one long edge, from the fold, one-half the measurement of the edge of the embroidery. Draw a line from this point to the corner. Cut away both corners.

Open out the pattern and use it to cut identical strips of fabric for each side of the border. If making a rectangular border, you will need to measure and cut a second paper pattern for the two shorter sides.

Trim the unworked canvas edges of the needlework to the same width as the seam allowance: 2cm (¾in).

Join the inner edge of each strip to one edge of the embroidery, placing right sides together and stitching either by machine or by hand (using backstitch), just inside the edge of the stitched area. Press the strips away from the embroidery.

Turn under and press the small seam allowance on each diagonal edge. Place the adjacent diagonal edges together and tack then stitch close to the crease line.

The rich patterning of this design is reminiscent of Victorian tapestry, but the colouring is much lighter. Worked in several shades of grey, the birds stand out clearly against the colourful background.

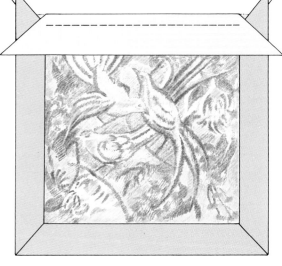

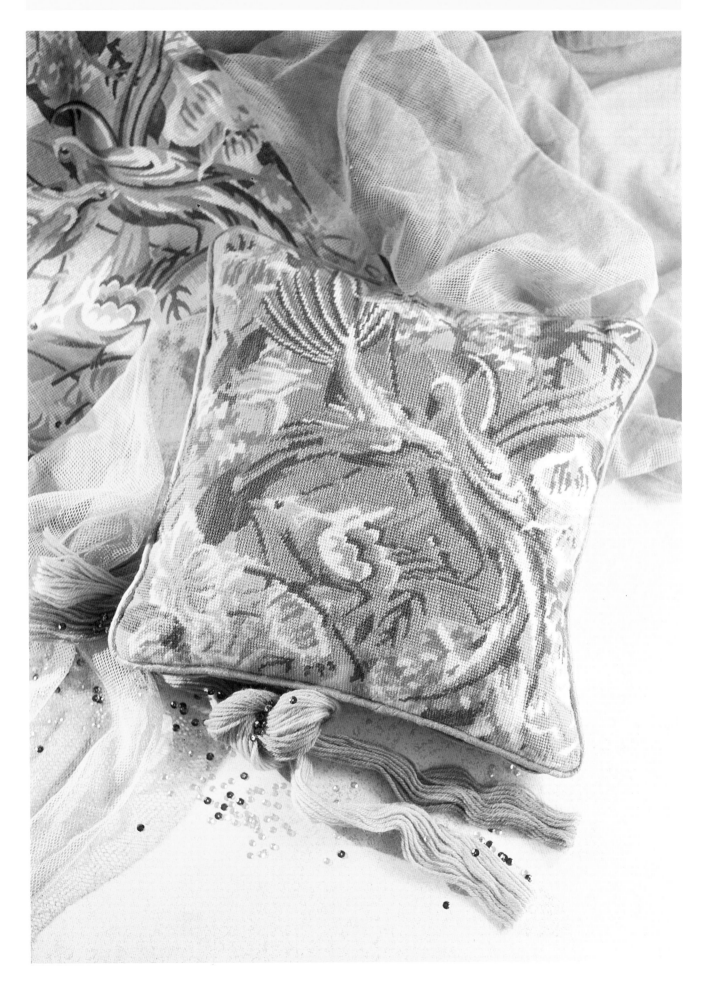

COLOURWAYS
FOR THREE
BIRDS

Ap991 (PA260)   *a*

Ap461 (PA564)   *b*

Ap462 (PA545)   *c*

Ap427 (PA644)   *d*

Ap961 (PA465)   *e*

Ap962 (PA203)   *f*

Ap963 (PA202)   *g*

Ap945 (PO904)   *h*

Ap753 (PA934)   *i*

Ap471 (PA727)   *j*

Ap352 (PA687)   *k*

Ap631 (PD501)   *l*

Ap427 (PA630)   *m*

Ap = Appleton
PA or PO or PD =
Paterna

Yarn amounts

a	38m	(42yd)
b	9m	(10yd)
c	20m	(22yd)
d	13m	(15yd)
e	24m	(27yd)
f	30m	(33yd)
g	27m	(30yd)
h	11m	(12yd)
i	15m	(17yd)
j	32m	(35yd)
k	10m	(11yd)
l	21m	(23yd)
m	13m	(15yd)

Materials

Tapestry wool (see colourways). The amounts given are calculated for half-cross stitch. To work the design in basketweave or continental tent, increase all amounts by 50 per cent. If either of these stitches is used, an ordinary mono canvas may be substituted for double thread or interlock. Two strands of Persian wool or three strands of crewel can be substituted for the single strand of tapestry wool used for this design.

12-gauge double or mono interlock canvas 45cm (18in) square
Size 18 tapestry needle
50cm (20in) furnishing fabric for backing
1.6m (5½ft) narrow piping cord
Cushion 38cm (15in) square
30cm (12in) zip fastener (optional)
Slate or stretcher frame (optional)
Tools and materials for preparing canvas (see page 10) and for blocking (page 11).

The finished cushion measures 37cm (14½in) square.

Working the embroidery

Prepare the canvas and mount it on the frame, if used (see page 10).

Following the chart on the left, work the design in half-cross stitch (or basketweave or continental tent stitch).

Blocking and making up

Block the completed work (see page 11) and allow it to dry thoroughly. Trim the canvas edges, leaving margins 2cm (¾in).

From the backing fabric cut a piece 41cm (16½in) square. Or, if inserting a zip, cut two pieces as specified on page 16.

From the remaining fabric, cut and join bias strips to cover the piping cord (see page 48).

If adding a zip, insert in the back cover.

Attach the piping to the back cover as described on page 48.

Join the front and back covers as described on page 16, and insert the cushion.

Shells

The striking composition featuring shells and seaside flowers has an other-worldly feeling with its clear, graphic outlines and star-speckled background.

Shells are an ideal subject for needle-point as they offer such a variety of colour and shape. (Kaffe Fassett often uses scallop shells as a corner motif.) They are found embroidered in delicate threads on bags, gloves and clothes in almost any textile museum or in bold outlines on hangings and carpets. Beside the intrinsic beauty of their shapes they have a romantic associ-ation with the shore and the beach that features in most people's childhood memories.

Sir Isaac Newton surveying his life wrote: 'I do not know what I may appear to the world, but to myself I seem to have been only a boy playing on the sea-shore, and diverting myself in now and then finding a smoother pebble or a prettier shell than ordinary, whilst the great ocean of truth lay all undiscovered before me.' For most of us the sea-shore retains a certain magic of play

and discovery and the exquisite shapes of shells and stones washed by the sea still act as artistic inspiration to artists and needle-workers alike.

Variations

Any of the shells in this tapestry could be taken separately, recoloured, regrouped or placed on softer backgrounds to provide an endless variety of subjects to stitch.

To adapt the design for a chair seat, you will need to eliminate the blue and yellow borders, since the chair seat will probably not be square but trapezoidal in shape (see page 27). Instead, fill the surrounding area with a solid, contrasting colour, using tent stitch, half-cross, or upright Gobelin over two threads. Instructions for covering a chair seat are given on pages 24-7.

Shells immediately evoke the sea and beach, and this design, like many of the square canvases in the book, would make a beautiful shoulder bag – although perhaps too good for anything but the most sophisticated beach party!

OTHER IDEAS

Shells are good subject matter for needlework and allow the use of a fresh, seaside palette of colours. Susan Skeen's sharp use of colour is well suited to this theme and she has mixed some unexpected pastels with the stronger blue and yellow.

To make a simple shoulder bag

In addition to the worked canvases for the front and back sections of the bag, you will need:

7.5cm (3in) wide upholstery webbing
  Measure the distance around three sides of the embroidery plus enough for a strap; the total should be about 2m (6½ft)

lining fabric: enough for twice the depth of the bag, plus gusset (see below) and seams

firm iron-on interfacing for front and back canvases

After blocking the embroidery, turn under and press the unworked canvas edges, mitring the corners (see page 122). Cut two pieces of interfacing to fit and iron them to the wrong side of each piece.

Cut two pieces of lining fabric the dimen-sions of the finished work plus 2cm (¾in) all round. Also cut a strip for the gusset,

11cm (4½in) wide by the distance round three sides of the work plus 4cm (1½in). Depending on the width of the fabric and the length required, the gusset may need to be pieced together.

Pin, tack and stitch the gusset around three sides of one lining section, taking 2cm (¾in) seam allowance. Then similarly join the free edge of the gusset to the other lining section. Press the seams open and put the lining aside.

Join the ends of the webbing by overlap-ping them by 2cm (¾in) and stitch firmly by machine or by hand. Place this join at the centre lower edge of one embroidered piece and, using strong thread, slipstitch one edge of the webbing round three sides of one bag section. Then slipstitch the other edge to the other section.

Insert the lining, wrong side outside, into the bag. Turn under the raw edges and slipstitch them to the top edge of the bag and webbing.

COLOURWAYS
FOR SHELLS

Ap882 (PA655)	*a*
Ap326 (PA510)	*b*
Ap206 (PD275)	*c*
Ap526 (PD501)	*d*
Ap752 (PA964)	*e*
Ap151 (PA901)	*f*
Ap202 (PA406)	*g*
Ap884 (PA325)	*h*
Ap561 (PA585)	*i*
Ap471 (PA704)	*j*
Ap204 (PA223)	*k*
Ap874 (PA624)	*l*

Ap = Appleton
PA or PD = Paterna

Yarn amounts

a	30m	(33yd)
b	69m	(76yd)
c	14m	(16yd)
d	14m	(16yd)
e	15m	(17yd)
f	13m	(15yd)
g	13m	(15yd)
h	18m	(20yd)
i	59m	(65yd)
j	59m	(65yd)
k	10m	(11yd)
l	10m	(11yd)

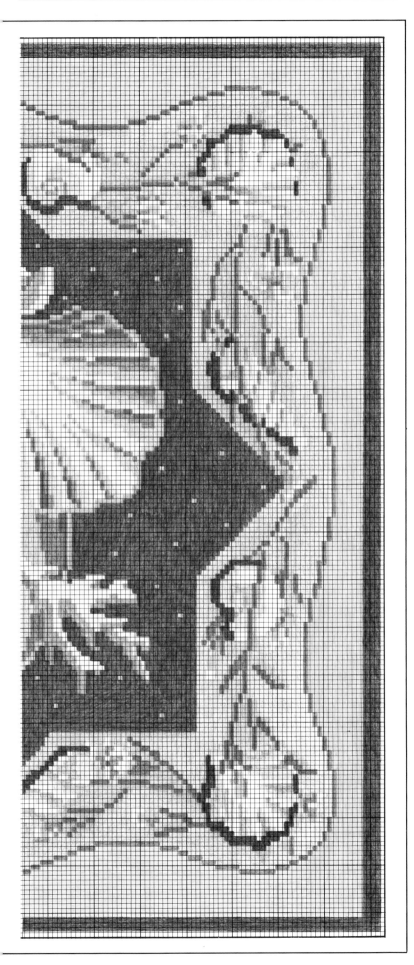

Materials
Tapestry wool (see colourways). The amounts given are calculated for half-cross stitch. To work the design in basketweave or continental tent, increase all amounts by 50 per cent. If either of these stitches is used, an ordinary mono canvas may be substituted for double thread or interlock. Two strands of Persian wool or three strands of crewel can be substituted for the single strand of tapestry wool used for this design.
14-mesh canvas 45cm (18in) square
Size 20 tapestry needle
40cm (16in) furnishing fabric for backing
1.6m (5½ft) narrow piping cord
Cushion 35cm (14in) or 38cm (15in)
    square
30cm (12in) zip fastener (optional)
Slate or stretcher frame (optional)
Tools and materials for preparing fabric
    (see page 10) and for blocking.

The finished cushion measures 35cm (14in) square.

Working the embroidery
Prepare the canvas and mount it on the frame, if used (see page 10).
    Following the chart on the left, work the design in half-cross stitch (or basketweave or continental tent stitch).

Blocking and making up
Block the completed work (see page 11) and allow it to dry thoroughly. Trim the canvas edges, leaving margins of 2cm (¾in).
    From the backing fabric cut a piece 39cm (15½in) square. Or, if inserting a zip, cut two pieces as specified on page 16, and follow instructions for zip.
    From the remaining fabric, cut and join bias strips to cover the piping cord (see page 48). Attach the piping to the back cover.
    Join the front and back covers as described on page 16, and insert the cushion.

Seashore Garland

A garland of stylized seaside flowers and shells, worked in rich pastel colours, is perfectly set off by the deep navy background of this little cushion.

Garlands have featured in needlework designs for centuries – summer flowers being a traditional favourite. But here Susan Skeen has continued to play upon the sea element by having her shells nestle among living anemones and sea holly.

The design was originally made for a workbox top (for which a kit is available, see pages 82 and 127), an interesting idea for many of the rectangular designs in this book.

Materials
Tapestry wool (see colourways). The amounts given are calculated for half-cross stitch. To work the design in basketweave or continental tent, increase all amounts by 50 per cent. If either of these stitches is used, an ordinary mono canvas may be substituted for double thread or interlock. Two strands of Persian wool or three strands of crewel can be substituted for the single strand of tapestry wool used for this design.

12-gauge double or mono interlock canvas, 45×35cm (18×14in)

Size 18 tapestry needle

40cm (16in) furnishing fabric for backing

1.4m (4½ft) narrow piping cord

Cushion pad 33×27cm (13×10in) or slightly larger (or calico and polyester filling to make a pad)

20cm (8in) zip fastener (optional)

Slate or stretcher frame (optional)

Tools and materials for preparing canvas (see page 10) and for blocking (page 11).

The finished cushion measures 33×27cm (13×10in).

Working the embroidery
Prepare the canvas and mount it on the frame, if used (see page 10).

Following the chart overleaf, work the design in half-cross stitch (or basketweave or continental tent stitch).

Blocking and making up
Block the completed work (see page 11) and allow it to dry thoroughly. Trim the canvas edges, leaving margins of 2cm (¾in).

From the backing fabric cut a piece 37cm

wide by 31cm deep (14½×12½in). Or, if inserting a zip, cut two pieces as specified on page 16.

From the remaining fabric, cut and join bias strips to cover the piping cord (see page 48).

Insert the zip, if desired, in the back cover.

Attach the piping to the back cover as described on page 48.

Join the front and back covers as described on page 16, and insert the cushion.

Making your own cushion pad

If you cannot find a cushion pad of the required size, make one from calico and polyester filling. Cut a piece of calico measuring 60×40cm (24×16in). Fold it in half, right sides and short edges together, and stitch around the open sides, taking 2cm (¾in) seam allowance, and leaving a gap of about 10cm (4in) for the filling. Turn the cushion right side out and insert the filling, working it well into the corners. Slipstitch the edges of the opening together.

Garlands are an ever-popular theme and in this cushion an unusual mixture of shells and flowers is used. The plain background makes it relatively easy to substitute your own choice of colour. Always remember, however, to check that the edge of the garland will not be lost in a different background colour.

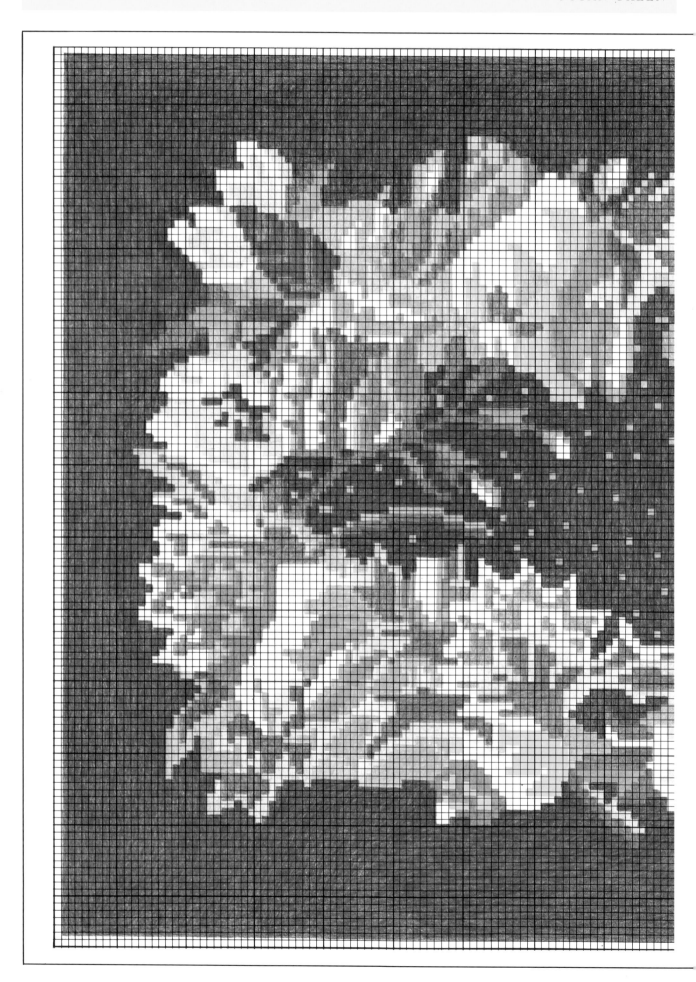

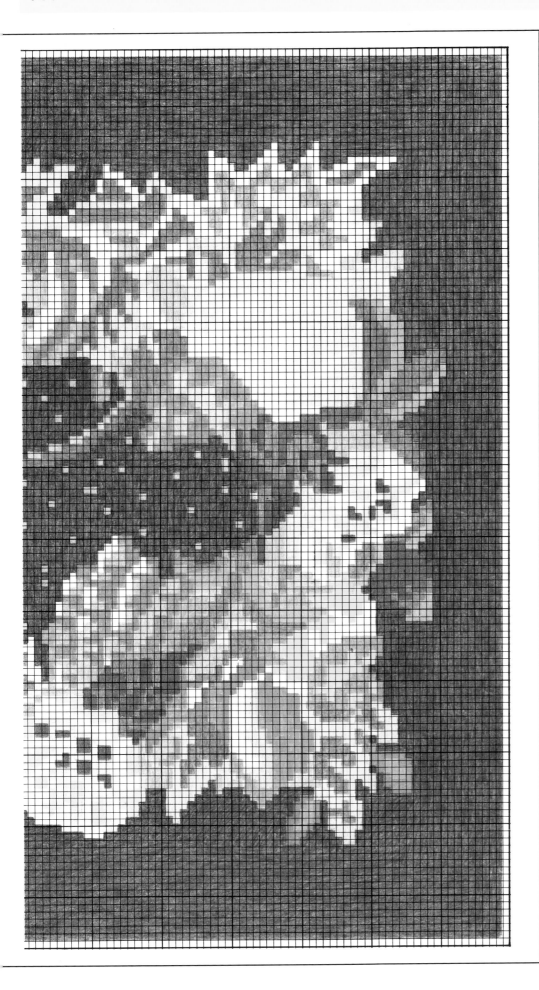

COLOURWAYS FOR SEASHORE GARLAND

Ap927 (PA571) *a*

Ap522 (PA595) *b*

Ap992 (PA262) *c*

Ap961 (PA204) *d*

Ap331 (PA735) *e*

Ap355 (PA602) *f*

Ap543 (PA653) *g*

Ap141 (PA924) *h*

Ap222 (PA932) *i*

Ap224 (PA931) *j*

Ap714 (PA910) *k*

Ap842 (PA703) *l*

Ap313 (PA750) *m*

Ap101 (PA313) *n*

Ap = Appleton
PA = Paterna

Yarn amounts
a	62m	(68yd)
b	8m	(9yd)
c	14m	(16yd)
d	9m	(10yd)
e	7m	(8yd)
f	13m	(15yd)
g	4m	(5yd)
h	5m	(6yd)
i	8m	(9yd)
j	4m	(5yd)
k	4m	(5yd)
l	4m	(5yd)
m	7m	(8yd)
n	2m	(2yd)

Variations

This design lends itself to various uses. Having been originally designed for a workbox top, it is ideally suited to this purpose. You might need to adjust the overall dimensions to suit the box. Or you could use it for a rectangular footstool. See the instructions for covering a footstool pad given on pages 24-7.

Another possibility is to use the design for a petit point evening bag. Use fine-gauge canvas (16 or 18) and perle or stranded cotton, or stranded silk and add tiny seed pearls to the stars in the centre. Use black thread for the background. It is best to make the bag to suit a particular frame and have it made up professionally. Frames are available from many needlework shops, and such places sometimes provide a making-up service.

If you prefer to make a larger cushion, you could work it in cross stitch on slightly finer canvas. For example, if you used 18-gauge canvas and worked the cross stitch for every square on the chart, the finished work would measure approximately 42cm wide by 35cm deep (16½×14in).

EDWIN BELCHAMBER

Edwin Belchamber studied at Eastbourne School of Art and Design and then at Hornsey College of Art where he received his Diploma of Art and Design specializing in graphics.

Although graphic design is the field in which he still does most of his work, including designing for publishers, advertising agencies and exhibitions, he has also produced some unusually interesting three-dimensional work. This has led him to experiment in various and often unexpected media, even cake, which he has used to create a number of fantastic sculptures. More recently he has also turned his artistry to garden design, and to needlepoint.

'Tapestry design is a new departure for me,' he says, 'one which I find interesting because it offers a chance to combine simple picture-making with the use of pattern.' Both of the designs reproduced here, Walled Garden and Lily Pond, are models in the use of perspective, and the carefully calculated balance of each picture reflects his interest and training in graphic design.

Lily Pond and Walled Garden

Both these designs are inspired by the gardens at Sissinghurst in Kent. The rose and morning-glory borders are designed to pick up the colours used in the scenes.

Sissinghurst Castle has one of the most photographed and visited gardens in the country. It is not a castle at all, although there is a sixteenth-century tower, but a group of buildings around which Harold Nicolson and his wife, Vita Sackville-West, created a garden in the 1930s. He was the designer and she the planter. It is famous for the colour schemes within each enclosure. The original combinations of plants ensure that in every season one section of the garden, at least, looks interesting. It is informally planted, and what Vita Sackville-West wrote about Hidcote in 1949 could equally well apply to Sissinghurst: 'A rumpus of colour, a drunkenness of scents.'

Walled Garden appropriately has a border of roses. Sissinghurst's roses are

legendary. Old French roses like 'Charles de Mills', 'Cardinal de Richelieu', 'Céleste', 'Fantin Latour' or 'Camieux' thrive in the heavy soil and free-grown bushes are often trained into old trees or round supports in a luxurious fashion. In June the riot of colour looks wonderful.

Another very good time to visit Sissinghurst is in the spring when the pleached Lime Walk is covered in a mass of small bulbs – narcissi, tulips, scillas, crocuses, fritillaries, anemones, and many others. After the Lime Walk you come to the nuttery, famous for its carpet of mixed polyanthus and further on is the Cottage Garden which is a warm assortment of yellow, red and orange flowers grouped around a verdigris-tinted old copper. In July the Mount Etna broom hangs over everything in a shower of tiny yellow flowers. The old moat was mostly drained but the waterfilled

parts stretch from the neat Herb Garden, round the Orchard to the White Garden.

The walls are covered in most unusual plants including blue poppies, and various urns and vases are placed at vantage points just as in Walled Garden.

The first garden laid out in this fashion was Hidcote, which Lawrence Johnston designed in 1905. Its design and planting has had more influence on modern gardening than any other. If Hidcote inspired the lay-out, the ideas of Gertrude Jekyll inspired the planting. She was the first to advocate gradations of colour and was the arch-exponent of the sweeping herbaceous border. Marvellous examples of these can be seen at Bodnant, Powis Castle and Wakehurst. Sissinghurst exemplifies this period of English gardening and part of its appeal is that it remains intact, in the style in which it was created.

These two pictures are a fascinating use of graphic design. The pictures were first drawn in meticulous detail, with the colour added afterwards. This has produced a stereoscopic clarity. Most of the other designs in this book have a flat, textural quality but these two, in complete contrast, hardly look stitched at all. They are exercises in perspective and as such make perfect pictures on a wall.

**COLOURWAYS
FOR LILY POND**

Ap465 (PA571)   *a*

Ap822 (PA542)   *b*

Ap461 (PA563)   *c*

Ap545 (PA602)   *d*

Ap252 (PA653)   *e*

Ap406 (PA610)   *f*

Ap761 (PA454)   *g*

Ap123 (PA404)   *h*

Ap955 (PA431)   *i*

Ap159 (PA530)   *j*

Ap991 (PA260)   *k*

Ap = Appleton
PA = Paterna

Yarn amounts

a	4m	(5yd)
b	9m	(10yd)
c	19m	(21yd)
d	28m	(31yd)
e	19m	(21yd)
f	47m	(52yd)
g	46m	(51yd)
h	12m	(13yd)
i	4m	(5yd)
j	19m	(21yd)
k	6m	(7yd)

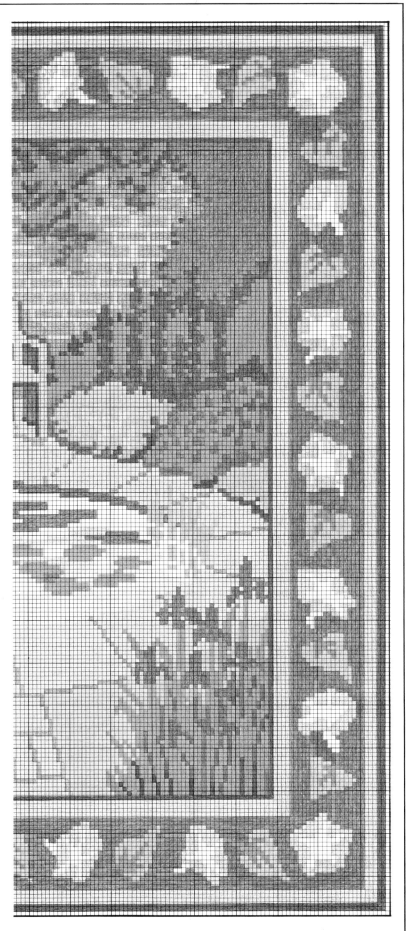

Materials

Tapestry wool (see colourways). The amounts given are calculated for half-cross stitch. To work the design in basketweave or continental tent, increase all amounts by 50 per cent. If either of these stitches is used, an ordinary mono canvas may be substituted for double or interlock. Two strands of Persian wool or three strands of crewel can be substituted for the single strand of tapestry wool used for this design.

12-gauge double or mono interlock canvas
    45cm (18in) square
Size 18 tapestry needle
Sheet stiff cardboard 37cm (15½in) square
Strong thread for lacing
Slate or stretcher frame (optional)
Tools and materials for preparing canvas
    (see page 10) and for blocking (page 11).

The finished panel, excluding the frame, measures 37cm (15½in) square.

Working the embroidery

Prepare the canvas and mount it on the frame, if used (see page 10).

Following the chart on the left, work the design in half-cross stitch (or basketweave or continental tent stitch).

Blocking and making up

Block the completed work (see page 11) and allow it to dry thoroughly. Do not trim the canvas edges.

Lace the work over the stiff cardboard (as described on page 68), ready for framing by a professional.

Materials

Tapestry wool (see colourways). The amounts given are calculated for half-cross stitch. To work the design in basketweave or continental tent, increase all amounts by 50 per cent. If either of these stitches is used, an ordinary mono canvas may be substituted for double thread or interlock. Two strands of Persian wool or three strands of crewel can be substituted for the single strand of tapestry wool used for this design.

12-gauge double or mono interlock canvas
    45cm (18in) square
Size 18 tapestry needle
Piece of stiff cardboard 37cm (15½in)
    square
Strong thread for lacing
Slate or stretcher frame (optional)
Tools and materials for preparing canvas
    (see page 10) and for blocking (page 11).

The finished panel, excluding the frame, measures 37cm (15½in) square.

Working the embroidery

Prepare the canvas and mount it on the frame, if used, (see page 10).

Following the chart on the right, work the design in half-cross stitch (or basketweave or continental tent stitch).

Blocking and making up

Block the completed work (see page 11) and allow it to dry thoroughly. Do not trim the canvas edges.

Lace the work over the stiff cardboard as described on page 68, so that it is ready to be professionally framed.

COLOURWAYS FOR WALLED GARDEN

Ap753 (PD281) *a*

Ap461 (PA564) *b*

Ap406 (PA610) *c*

Ap252 (PA653) *d*

Ap545 (PA602) *e*

Ap761 (PA454) *f*

Ap206 (PA862) *g*

Ap302 (PA435) *h*

Ap159 (PA530) *i*

Ap991 (PA260) *j*

Ap955 (PD123) *k*

Ap = Appleton
PA or PD = Paterna

Yarn amounts

a	10m	(11yd)
b	8m	(9yd)
c	37m	(41yd)
d	28m	(31yd)
e	37m	(41yd)
f	46m	(51yd)
g	11m	(12yd)
h	21m	(23yd)
i	10m	(11yd)
j	23m	(26yd)
k	31m	(34yd)

Variations

The rose motif used for the border of Walled Garden could be used on its own to make a handsome cushion with a formal arrangement of roses. Select a section of three roses and repeat it four times across the cushion. If you double the size, by working four stitches for each one shown on the guide, the work will measure roughly 40cm (16in) deep. The width can be varied to suit your taste, or the size of cushion available, by increasing or reducing the space to either side of the flowers or by adjusting the width of the plain stripe between motifs.

You can substitute textural variety for some of the linear interest in this panel by using a variety of stitches. Work the sky, for example, in rows of two shades of blue plus white, incorporating short lines of wide Gobelin (page 13); work the trees and foreground shrubs in cross stitch (page 13) (some of the detail will have to be sacrificed); the grass in encroaching Gobelin (page 13) over 3 threads; the edges of the steps in upright Gobelin (page 13) over 3 threads and the steps in slanted Gobelin (page 13) over 2 threads. Work the patterned parts of the wall in brick stitch in one or two shades of brown (leaving the shaded parts of the wall and all other details, in half-cross or tent stitch). To work brick stitch:

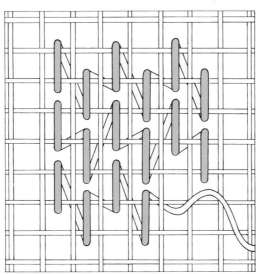

Finally, work over the flowers with French knots to bring them forwards. Working the leaves and flowers in shiny cotton thread will help to accentuate them. To work a French knot:

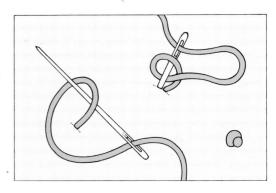

A variety of stitches would add textural interest. For example: work the wall of either picture in brick stitch, using two shades of brown; the bench in upright Gobelin (page 13) over two threads, worked both vertically and horizontally; the shrubs in cross stitch (page 13); to suggest the flowers in the shrubs, work some of the cross stitches in blue. The water of the lily pond could be suggested by continental tent stitch, mixing in short lines of wide Gobelin (page 13) and using blue, green and white randomly; work the paving in flat stitch (page 115) over 3 threads; the grass in encroaching slanted Gobelin (page 13); and the reeds and irises in tent stitch. On top of the ten stitch work lines of stem stitch (page 38) and detached chain stitches, as appropriate, to accentuate these details.

To work detached chain stitches:

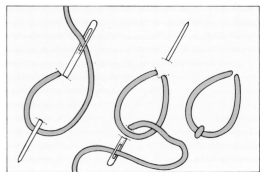

VICTORIA & ALBERT MUSEUM

The Victoria and Albert Museum in London is Britain's leading museum for the decorative arts, and among its many collections of decorative objects is the famous collection of embroideries. Most notable are the English embroideries which include the Bradford Table Carpet, the fourteenth-century Syon Cope, and the panels from the Oxburgh hanging worked by Mary, Queen of Scots and Elizabeth, Countess of Shrewsbury. There are also innumerable covers, samplers and chair seats, not to mention a wonderful selection of medieval woven wallhangings.

With such a width of choice it is often difficult to know where to start and many of the tapestry designs used in this book are in fact based on sections taken from carpets, painted manuscripts or textiles. The joy of the museum is in the richness of its range. Under Sir Roy Strong the Victoria and Albert Museum has revived its lapsed tradition of supporting contemporary craftsmen and designers: Kaffe Fassett and Susan Duckworth are among those whose work has recently been purchased. In this way the tradition and continuity of the particular crafts are carried through to the present day and contribute greatly to the colour and vitality of this magnificent institution.

Carnations

The Victoria and Albert Museum has among its many treasures, a very fine collection of Indian miniatures and manuscripts. The stylized flowers in this cushion are taken from a border of a Mughal manuscript dating from about 1635 and we have simplified the colours and repeated the flower to produce a harmonious, symmetrical design. This type of Indian flower decoration originated in Persia but flowered under the patronage of Imperial Mughal rule from 1550 to 1850 when there was almost continuous employment for artists at the courts of Agra, Delhi or Lahore and at the palaces of the provincial nobility. Floral borders, like the one 'carnation' has been adapted from, often surrounded miniature portraits for animal studies and were bound in albums. They were for contemplation and their own intrinsic beauty and could almost be described as the coffee table books of the day. Naturally they are a visual feast and individual flower motifs lend themselves to endless pattern combinations.

The flowering plant became a dominant theme in all types of decoration after Jahangir's ecstatic experiences of the Kashmir Flora in 1620 and, curiously, the movement drew further inspiration from European herbal studies which had reached the Mughal Court. In 1982 the Victoria and Albert Museum put together an outstanding exhibition of their Indian art and their catalogue, 'The Indian Heritage', describes and illustrates the plethora of floral motifs found in all branches of Indian decorative art. They appear in carpets, textile embroideries and as decoration on Mughal buildings, such as the Taj Mahal.

The glory of these Indian flower patterns is their adaptability. You can design a canvas of almost any size and shape by juggling them around to suit your requirements. A piano stool, for example, could easily be worked out by simply extending the top and bottom row of flowers and repeating the central flower as many times as is necessary to suit the length of the stool. Also, colouring can be adapted with great ease – almost like 'paint-by-numbers'. Try alternate colouring for the flowers in the border and experiment with different background colours. We here chose a cream and a deep blue as our backgrounds, but deep red, black or pale biscuit-brown could look equally good. The only thing to watch is that the colours of the flowers which edge the background do not blend into it. A bottle green would be difficult for this reason. This really is a design to play around with and if you are recolouring a canvaswork design for the first time this would be an ideal one to start with. Of course there is no need to stick with naturalistic colours – the most surprising combinations can often produce an attractive and original design.

This advice holds good for almost any needlepoint design in this book. If you see one particular motif you really like, whether it be a flower, an animal, a vase or almost anything, extract it from the overall design, repeat it and start playing around with combinations of the motif. You will be astonished how successful this can be and some of the nicest textile designs are simply repeat patterns of one particular motif. Look through the designs in this book again and you will find enough individual motifs to last you a lifetime. Do not be put off by the complexity of many of the overall pictures – try to imagine you are a surgeon and just cut out and extract any motif that appeals to you from the jungle of pattern and colour.

Variations

You could use the central motif for a pretty little picture. Use finger-gauge canvas – 16 or 18 – and perle cotton thread. You could add a border to the design, perhaps using two or three lines of upright Gobelin (page 13) in pink and green.

A piano bench seat could use the small motifs scattered randomly over a black background, with slightly lighter shades of green used for the stems and leaves.

For a pretty patch pocket for a skirt, work the central motif in cross stitch on even-weave linen or cotton fabric. Note that the motif is asymmetrical, so should be reversed if you wish to make two pockets. An evenweave with 32 threads to 2.5cm (1in) will produce a cross-stitched motif measuring approximately 11cm wide by 12cm high (4½×4¾in).

One of the simplest designs in this book and one of the most versatile for 'redesigning'. A variety of background colours could be substituted, so this is a design to play around with to suit your own taste and colour requirements.

COLOURWAYS FOR CARNATIONS

Ap947 (PA941)   *a*

Ap944 (PA904)   *b*

Ap942 (PA934)   *c*

Ap623 (PA822)   *d*

Ap621 (PA865)   *e*

Ap881 (PA948)   *f*

Ap406 (PA690)   *g*

Ap543 (PA693)   *h*

Ap993 (PA220)   *i*

Ap743 (PA562)   *j*

The alternative background colour shown for this cushion on page 93 is Ap324 (PA551)

Ap = Appleton
PA = Paterna

Yarn amounts

a	2m	(2yd)
b	7m	(8yd)
c	9m	(10yd)
d	6m	(7yd)
e	10m	(11yd)
f	175m	(193yd)
g	19m	(21yd)
h	20m	(22yd)
i	2m	(2yd)
j	1m	(1yd)

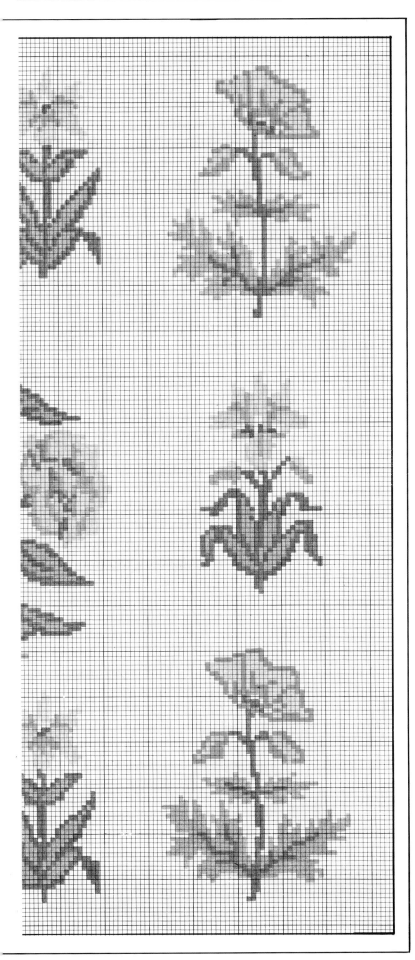

Materials

Tapestry wool (see colourways). The amounts given are calculated for half-cross stitch. To work the design in basketweave or continental tent, increase all amounts by 50 per cent. If either of these stitches is used, an ordinary mono canvas may be substituted for double thread or interlock. Two strands of Persian wool or three strands of crewel can be substituted for the single strand of tapestry wool used for this design.

12-gauge double or mono interlock canvas
    50cm (20in) square
Size 18 tapestry needle
50cm (20in) furnishing fabric for backing
1.8m (6ft) narrow piping cord
Cushion 40cm (16in) square
35cm (14in) zip fastener (optional)
Slate or stretcher frame (optional)
Tools and materials for preparing canvas
    (see page 10) and for blocking (page 11).

The finished cushion measures 40cm (16in) square.

Working the embroidery

Prepare the canvas and mount it on the frame, if used (see page 10).

Following the chart on the left, work the design in half-cross stitch (or basketweave or continental tent stitch).

Blocking and making up

Block the completed work (see page 11) and allow it to dry thoroughly. Trim the canvas edges, leaving margins of 2cm (¾in).

From the backing fabric cut a piece 44cm (17½in) square. Or, if inserting a zip, cut two pieces as specified on page 16.

From the remaining fabric, cut and join bias strips to cover the piping cord (see page 48). Make up the piping.

If using a zip, insert in the back cover.

Attach the piping to the back cover as described on page 48.

Join the front and back covers as described on page 16, and insert the cushion.

Elephant

This seemed a perfect subject for a jolly children's cushion. It also has the simplicity and subtle colouring which should appeal to adults as well. In the original wall-hanging, from which this cushion is adapted, elephants, soldiers and animals all parade across the picture in a gloriously haphazard fashion. We took a particularly appealing elephant and surrounded him with a random selection of soldiers, birds and musicians taken from the hanging. Once again we have taken motifs from a larger picture and rearranged them. We have also recoloured the background in the warm cherry red, changing it from a pale beige in the original. The colouring of the figures, however, is taken from the original.

The wall-hanging is on public display in the museum and is well worth a visit. It is stitched with silk, in satin stitch on a cotton background, and came from the Palace of Chamba. It depicts the battle of Kurukshetra as described in the Mahabharata epic. The Mahabharata, like the more commonly known Ramayana, is an epic poem of India's origins – in fact it is the world's longest poem. In so far as it has any historical connection it belongs to several centuries from about 1000 BC and its location is generally thought to centre around the Ganges basin. The embroidery, however, dates from the late eighteenth century and the costumes are contemporary to the work.

Elephants were a popular theme in both Indian textiles and carpets. They were used for hunting as well as fighting and for all types of ceremonial procession. The Mughal emperors and their courts were always on the move – like mediaeval European monarchs – and we are told by Abu'l Fazl that a short journey required 500 camels, 400 carts, 100 bearers, 500 troopers, numerous officials, 1000 labourers, 500 pioneers (whose job it was to level the selected site), 100 water-carriers, 50 carpenters, tent-makers and torch-bearers, 30 leatherworkers, 150 sweepers and, to complement the party, 100 elephants. When the procession came to rest, vast numbers of tents were then erected and since this 'camp' would be a temporary court, rich carpets, silken cushions and

hangings would have been brought to decorate the tents. Many of the most beautiful surviving embroideries from this period were used as tent-hangings.

India, along with China, was always the world's most famous source of luxury textiles. The Greeks and Romans admired Indian cottons, in particular the transparent 'Gangetic Muslins' of Banares and Bengal and later Indian chintzes, dyed cottons, silks and ikats were all highly prized in the West. The traditions of embroidery were equally well-established and by the seventeenth century imperial workshops had been set up in the cities of Lahore, Agra and Ahmedabad for the best local craftsmen to supply the needs of the court. Such workshops were also attached to the courts of the leading princes and there was both a carpet factory and a workshop with thirty-six separate departments at Amber.

Variations
The different motifs on this cushion can be used singly or combined in various ways. The central motif of the elephant and riders could be used for a picture, perhaps with the background worked in kelim (page 38), flat (page 115) or upright Gobelin (page 13) stitch. Add a border of grey and cream in a stitch of your choice.

The warriors and musicians could be used individually for striking bookmarks. Use 18-gauge canvas and two strands of crewel or one strand of Persian wool. You could add the initials of the person for whom the bookmark is intended, working them out on graph paper first. For the lining use imitation or real suede or felt, none of which requires neatening.

The border figures are also ideal for a frieze for a child's bedroom or playroom, to go around the edges of the cot or along a wall. If you are placing the frieze near the ceiling, use 10-gauge canvas to make the figures larger; or use a finer-canvas and work in cross stitch over two threads.

If you are making the cushion and wish the border figures to be more prominent – or to enlarge the size of the cushion – add a fabric border of 4 or 5cm (2in). See the instructions for making a fabric border on page 70.

The elephant, birds and soldiers were extracted from a wall hanging in the Victoria and Albert Museum and arranged to make this cushion cover. We added a deep cherry background to give the design a warm, cheerful feeling. Although originally intended as a cushion for a child's room it would also look good with oriental carpets, ikats or rich, red fabrics.

COLOURWAYS FOR ELEPHANT

Ap153 (PA534) *a*

Ap322 (PA512) *b*

Ap503 (PA951) *c*

Ap584 (PA421) *d*

Ap691 (PA755) *e*

Ap901 (PA414) *f*

Ap947 (PA951) *g*

Ap987 (PA465) *h*

Ap993 (PA220) *i*

Ap = Appleton
PA = Paterna

Yarn amounts

a	21m	(23yd)
b	13m	(14yd)
c	102m	(113yd)
d	6m	(7yd)
e	21m	(23yd)
f	14m	(16yd)
g	5m	(6yd)
h	10m	(11yd)
i	5m	(6yd)

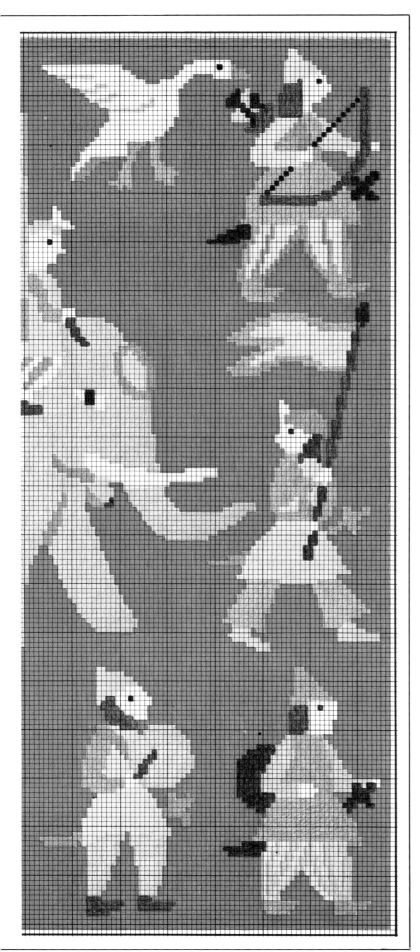

Materials

Tapestry wool (see colourways). The amounts given are calculated for half-cross stitch. To work the design in basketweave or continental tent, increase all amounts by 50 per cent. If either of these stitches is used, an ordinary mono canvas may be substituted for double thread or interlock. Two strands of Persian wool or three strands of crewel can be substituted for the single strand of tapestry wool used for this design.

12-gauge double or mono interlock canvas
    50cm (20in) square
Size 18 tapestry needle
50cm (20in) furnishing fabric for backing
1.6m (5½ft) narrow piping cord
Cushion 38cm (15in) square
35cm (14in) zip fastener (optional)
Slate or stretcher frame (optional)
Tools and materials for preparing canvas
    (see page 10) and for blocking (page 11).

The finished cushion measures 37cm (14½in) square.

Working the embroidery

Prepare the canvas and mount it on the frame, if used (see page 10).

Following the chart on the left, work the design in half-cross stitch (or basketweave or continental tent stitch).

Blocking and making up

Block the completed work (see page 11) and allow it to dry thoroughly. Trim the canvas edges, leaving margins of 2cm (¾in).

From the backing fabric cut a piece 41cm (16½in) square. Or, if inserting a zip, cut two pieces as specified on page 16.

From the remaining fabric, cut and join bias strips to cover the piping cord (see page 48). Make up the piping.

If adding a zip, insert in the back cover.

Attach the piping to the back cover as described on page 48.

Join the front and back covers as described on page 16, and insert the cushion.

The Harvesters

This picture is taken from a series depicting the 'labours of the months' woven as a tapestry panel. The panel is from Alsace, worked in a mixture of wool and linen and dates from the middle of the sixteenth century. It is on public display in the museum and would originally have hung over a wooden bench. It shows the labours of the months from July to December with the names of the months inscribed on scrolls over each theme: in July, peasants cut and gather the hay; in August the corn is reaped; September is for harvesting and sowing; October for cutting the grapes and making the wine; in November the ox is slaughtered; and finally in December they enjoy the fruits of their labour and sit eating at a table.

This was a recurrent medieval theme for a society where the weather and the harvest were all-important and dependent on the will of God. There are numerous medieval European paintings for the different seasons and their progress.

From the photograph on the right you will see that we have taken July, August and October to make individual pictures from the tapestry panel, and in time we hope to complete the series. They make charming naïve pictures and we have tried to reproduce their colours as faithfully as possible. The deep, warm colours of these tapestries look very good on walls and an enlarged version done on, say, seven-mesh canvas would make a striking wall-hanging. It is a fallacy to think that a medieval wall-hanging only looks in place with oak panelling and period furniture. They look lovely on almost any plain coloured, painted wall.

It would also be easy to reduce the size of the picture simply by using a finer-gauge canvas. If, for example, you chose an 18-gauge mesh, the picture would measure approximately 32×22cm (12½×8½in).

Materials

Tapestry wool (see colourways). The amounts given are calculated for half-cross stitch. To work the design in basketweave or continental tent, increase all amounts by 50 per cent. If either of these stitches is used, an ordinary mono canvas may be substituted for double thread or interlock. Two strands of Persian wool or three strands of crewel can be substituted for the single strand of tapestry wool used for this design.

14-gauge double or mono interlock canvas,

Medieval tapestry panels have great appeal with their naïve subject matter and earthy deep colouring. These three were originally from a long sixteenth-century panel depicting the labours of the months and they make excellent individual pictures.

50×40cm (20×16in)
Size 20 tapestry needle
Sheet stiff cardboard 41×28cm
     (16½×11in)
Strong thread for lacing
Slate or stretcher frame (optional)
Tools and materials for preparing
canvas (see page 10) and for blocking
     (page 11).

The finished panel, excluding the frame,
measures 41×28cm (16½×11in).

Working the embroidery

Prepare the canvas and mount it on the
frame, if used (see page 10).

Following the chart overleaf, work the
design in half-cross stitch (or basketweave
or continental tent stitch).

Blocking and making up

Block the completed work (see page 11)
and allow it to dry thoroughly. Do not trim
the edges. Lace the work over the stiff cardboard (see page 68) prior to framing.

COLOURWAYS FOR THE HARVESTERS

Ap203 (PA490) *a*

Ap224 (PD234) *b*

Ap503 (PA951) *c*

Ap841 (PA764) *d*

Ap694 (PA703) *e*

Ap988 (PA465) *f*

Ap303 (PD521) *g*

Ap341 (PA644) *h*

Ap354 (PA603) *i*

Ap158 (PA531) *j*

Ap746 (PA560) *k*

Ap328 (PA510) *l*

Ap = Appleton
PA or PD = Paterna

Yarn amounts

a	8m	(9yd)
b	12m	(13yd)
c	9m	(10yd)
d	10m	(11yd)
e	20m	(22yd)
f	5m	(6yd)
g	6m	(7yd)
h	12m	(13yd)
i	9m	(10yd)
j	57m	(63yd)
k	4m	(5yd)
l	68m	(75yd)

Vase Rug

This design has been very loosely based on a magnificent carpet, made of cotton and silk in 1850, which was originally in the palace at Amber in Rajasthan. The colours are quite different – the original is in deep reds and greens – but the vases with flowers were such appealing decorations for a carpet that we adapted them for this rug. Pale pastel colours look very good in modern interiors, with paler fabric and wallpaper colours, so we decided to colour this rug in a similar way and the original Mughal motif lends itself extremely well to this treatment. This rug would go particularly well in a bedroom and the pale colours would go with most neutral carpet colours. It also looks good on any type of wooden floor (as we photographed it) or for that matter on a light tiled floor. You could, of course, stitch it in any colours you like and the deep red of the original might act as a good background for recolouring. The flame-patterned, bargello-effect border would need to be recoloured in tune with whatever background colour was chosen, but the vases and flowers could look good as they are, on a variety of backdrops.

It seems surprising but there is no record of carpets being made in India before the mid-sixteenth century. The Victoria and Albert Museum think that the first weavers were imported from Herat, in present-day Afghanistan, which was still an important centre of Persian culture, and during the sixteenth and seventeenth centuries Persian influence on Mughal textiles, including carpets, was very strong.

The 'Amber' carpet is a series of inter-linked vases with flowers. For this rug we only had room for one of these motifs, as the originals are fairly detailed. However, you will notice that the design is not a mirror image: we took two distinct but very similar motifs and added a new border to complement the overall design. The original carpet has therefore been used only as an inspiration for this rug and it is in no sense an adaptation of the original.

The complexity of the patterning was also dictated by the technical requirements of the rug. We wanted a rug that was simple and quick to make and we have chosen a thick five-mesh canvas for this reason. The vase with its flowers is reminiscent of Kaffe Fassett's 'Caucasian Flower' cushion and it could be translated to a finer canvas to make a very attractive cushion itself. There has been a lack of good rug kits available for a long time and the flood of beautiful Portuguese rugs, Indian dhurries and modern carpet designs now available should act as an inspiration to needleworkers.

The rug could be scaled down, if desired, using rug canvas with – for example – 7 holes per 2.5cm (1in) and four strands of Persian wool; in this case the rug would measure about 80×58cm (32×23in).

You could use half of the rug design to make an attractive cushion. Worked on 10-gauge canvas with three strands of Persian, four of crewel or one of tapestry wool, the cushion would measure approximately 41cm wide by 28cm deep (16½×11in).

Materials

Rug yarn (see colourways). The amounts given are calculated for half-cross stitch. To work the design in basketweave or continental tent, increase all amounts by 50 per cent.
200m (220yd) double knitting-weight
    fringing yarn in cream
Piece of 5-gauge rug canvas 120×94cm
    (48×37½in)
1.2m (4ft) hessian (burlap) for backing
Strong linen thread
Size 3.5mm crochet hook
Tools and materials for preparing canvas
    (see page 10) and for blocking.
The finished rug measures 111×81cm (44½×32½in), excluding fringe.

Working the embroidery

Prepare the canvas as described on page 10. Few frames are large enough for this size project; and one that is large enough would be cumbersome to handle. You may find it most comfortable to work with the rug supported on a table.

Following the chart overleaf, work the design in half-cross stitch, or in basket-weave tent stitch. Continental tent *may* be used; however, because it distorts the canvas and because blocking a rug is hard work in any case, this stitch is not recommended.

A hardwearing rug stitched on 5-mesh canvas which would go just as well in a bedroom as in this hall. Its pale soft colouring was inspired by the numerous Indian dhurries now available in the shops.

COLOURWAYS FOR VASE RUG

36: 276m (301yd) 350gm

78: 20m (22yd) 25gm

86: 20m (22yd) 25gm

2: 158m (172yd) 200gm

44: 158m (172yd) 200gm

45: 158m (172yd) 200gm

40: 630m (688yd) 800gm

(Readicut rug wools)

Making up a rug

Block the completed work (see page 11), using an extra large board. Allow it to dry thoroughly; this may take several days.

After the canvas has been allowed to dry thoroughly, turn under the unworked edges and stitch in place with strong linen thread and oversewing. Mitre the corners.

At this point you may wish to fringe the short ends. Cut 632 strands of the fringing yarn, each approximately 30cm (12in) long. Using two strands together at a time, fold the strands double and pull them through one of the holes of the folded edges of the rug. With the crochet hook, take the strands through the loop as shown.

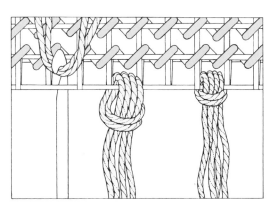

When all the strands have been attached, knot the first and third bunch of strands together, positioning the knot approximately 4cm (1½in) from the edge; then join the second and fifth, then the fourth and seventh, and so on, so that the strands overlap each other in a lattice. There are of course various more complicated knotting sequences that you can use (experiment first on a few strands hooked into a piece of spare canvas), but remember that these will take more yarn.

Instead of rug yarn, you could make a luxurious fringe out of a silken thread, doubling the strands to make up the thickness.

To calculate how much yarn to buy for a simpler fringe, first decide how long you would like your fringe to be. Add on 1cm (½in) for the knot and multiply by four (as each knot will be two strands doubled over) and then multiply by the number of holes along the ends to be fringed.

Line the rug with a piece of hessian (burlap), cut 2cm (¾in) larger than the finished rug, to allow for the seams. Turn under the seam on all edges, mitring the corners, and tack, then slipstitch the lining to the wrong side of the rug.

KAFFE FASSETT

Kaffe Fassett is rapidly becoming a household name. His prodigious output over the years has covered many different fields: wallpapers and fabrics for Designers' Guild, knitwear for Missoni of Italy, clothes with Bill Gibb, paintings and murals, not to mention his own knitting and tapestry designs. His book *Glorious Knitting* exploded on to the scene last year and became an instant bestseller. It was quite unlike any previous knitting book, with a standard of photography and presentation to match the knitting. 'Kaffe Fassett has a magical touch with colour, whether he is designing bold knitwear, working on a detailed needlepoint, mural or painting his vivid still lifes on canvas,' says Suzy Menkes, fashion editor of *The Times*, and Sir Roy Strong, the Director of the Victoria & Albert Museum recently described him as 'the genius of the knitting needle'.

Born in San Francisco, Kaffe Fassett studied fine art in Boston before moving to England in 1964. His work is in many important costume and textile collections through-out the world. He travels indefatigably conducting his immensely popular lectures and workshops on knitting and needlepoint, and his own book of new needlepoint designs will be published soon. Ehrman owe a special debt of gratitude to Kaffe Fassett as he inspired and encouraged them to produce their first tapestry kit and has remained over the years their principal designer.

Seabird

The distinctive border of this design was inspired by the highly decorated roof beams of old Chinese palaces. The original would have been in very bright red, blue, jade and gold, but the colours here are a more muted rendition which, as well as combining well with modern decoration, give the right emphasis to the central motif. The blues and greys edged with white form stylized waves round the ibis, and this detail too is often found in Chinese painting.

The slanting Chinese roof derived its style originally from Buddhist temples, as did the pagoda. The pagoda started as a simple one-storey building, like the Indian stupa, but the Chinese then added extra ones. They eventually reached twelve storeys and these were topped by a roof on branching bracketing which enabled the eaves to be extended far beyond the outer row of pillars. At this period an 'ang' was used in the roof structure. This is a slanting curved arm, reaching right out under the eaves, which was used as a lever bridging the two sets of bracketing. This clever means of construction was dropped in the Ming period when the roofs became narrower.

The Forbidden City, the palace and administrative city of the Emperor, has the most beautifully decorated roofs where the details of the woodwork are picked out in glowing colours. The glazed tiles on the roofs are yellow – brilliant yellow was the Emperor's own colour and could only be used by him – and the roof ridge ends are embellished with dragon finials. The capped ridges are decorated with symbolic animal tiles. From the fifteenth century onwards architectural techniques and design were static in China, and originality and inspiration found their expression in these very characteristic decorations.

Variations
Instead of a fabric border, you could work a plain embroidered border around the main design. For this you will need a piece of canvas 55cm (22in) square. You will also need additional wool in the chosen colour(s). (See page 70).

The easiest kind of border is one using half-cross, basketweave or continental stitch in one colour. You could vary this by using upright Gobelin stitch (page 13) over 2 or 3 threads. You could make all the rows of Gobelin horizontal, if you wish, so that they meet the design at right angles at the side edges. Or you could work all rows parallel to the edges, so that they form a 'mitred' effect at the corners.

The bird motif on its own could be used for a charming little picture. You could make it smaller by using finer canvas – perhaps 18-gauge, with one strand of perle cotton. Work a simple border of half-cross or tent stitch around the edges.

The wide border of this design would adapt beautifully to a bell pull. Work out the repeats on graph paper first, modifying the inner edges as necessary.

Birds have appeared in needlepoint designs throughout the centuries and remain one of the most appealing subjects. Kaffe Fassett's Chinese bird is unusual because of the scale of the border. It shows that the maximum amount of space for a picture does not necessarily create the maximum impact. The eye is immediately drawn to the bird because the border is so large and the central picture is surprisingly small.

OTHER IDEAS

Making a bell pull
Many needlework shops stock hardware specially designed for bell pulls; however, if you prefer you can simply buy a short length of dowelling for hanging it and a curtain ring to sew at the bottom. You will also need lining fabric and some iron-on interfacing.

The bell pull should be about 140-145cm long and 11 or 12cm wide (approximately 4½ft long and 4-5in wide). Make it slightly narrower than the shank of the hardware, to allow for the thickness of the embroidery.

After blocking the completed embroidery, turn under and press the trimmed canvas edges. Mitre the corners as shown on page 122. Apply a piece of iron-on interfacing to the wrong side, covering the edges. Cut the lining 2cm (¾in) larger than the embroidery all round. Turn under and press the edges, mitring the corners. Tack and then slipstitch the lining in place.

Attach the hardware following the manufacturer's instructions.

Materials

Tapestry wool (see colourways). The amounts given are calculated for half-cross stitch. To work the design in basketweave or continental tent, increase all amounts by 50 per cent. If either of these stitches is used, an ordinary mono canvas may be substituted for double thread or interlock. Three strands of Persian wool or four strands of crewel can be substituted for the single strand of tapestry wool used for this design.

10-gauge double or mono interlock canvas
    45cm (18in) square
Size 18 tapestry needle
60cm (24in) furnishing fabric for backing
2m (6½ft) narrow piping cord
Cushion 45cm (18in) square
40cm (16in) zip fastener (optional)
Slate or stretcher frame (optional)
Tools and materials for preparing canvas
    (see page 10) and for blocking (page 11)

The finished cushion measures approximately 45cm (18in) square; the embroidery, 36cm (14½in) square.

Working the embroidery

Prepare the canvas and mount it on the frame, if used (see page 10). Following the chart on the right, work the design in half-cross stitch (or basketweave or continental tent stitch).

Blocking and making up

Block the completed work (see page 11) and allow it to dry thoroughly. Trim the canvas edges, leaving margins of 2cm (¾in). Or, if inserting a zip, cut two pieces as instructed on page 16.

From the backing fabric cut a piece 50cm (20in) square. Also cut four strips for the border (see page 70), making them 50cm (20in) long on one edge, 40cm (16in) long on the opposite edge, and 9cm (3in) deep. Cut and join bias strips to cover the piping cord (see page 48).

Attach the border strips to the canvas as described on page 70.

Make up the piping and attach to the back cover as described on page 48.

If including a zip, insert at this stage, then join the front and back covers as described on page 16, and insert the cushion.

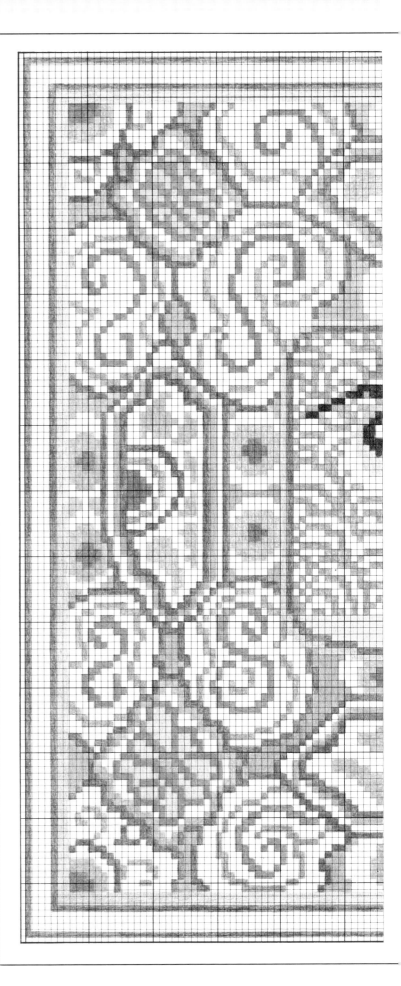

COLOURWAYS FOR SEABIRD

An0402 (PA260) *a*

An0403 (PA220) *b*

An0400 (PA200) *c*

An0412 (PA831) *d*

An0339 (PA882) *e*

An0859 (PA604) *f*

An0837 (PA525) *g*

An067 (PA934) *h*

An0160 (PA562) *i*

An0366 (PA805) *j*

An = Anchor
PA = Paterna

Yarn amounts

a	60m	(66yd)
b	10m	(11yd)
c	20m	(22yd)
d	10m	(11yd)
e	20m	(22yd)
f	20m	(22yd)
g	10m	(11yd)
h	10m	(11yd)
i	20m	(22yd)
j	10m	(11yd)

Peony Jar

Many of Kaffe Fassett's paintings are still lifes of China and these images appear in his wallpaper and textile designs.

He spotted the original of this jar – it is 2½ feet high – in a shop at Camden Lock, London, and was immediately thrilled by its shape and particularly its broad stripes. It has become a recurring theme in several of his designs and features in a huge canvas work over 8 feet high. The colouring of the jar itself is rawer, more vibrant than the gentle colours reproduced on the cushion.

These brighter colours were introduced to Chinese decorative art in the mid-eighteenth century under the Manchu emperors. In decoration a more varied palette was used, extending the range of colours found in Ming porcelain. Called *Famille Verte* by Europeans these pots were painted in the style of contemporary bird or flower paintings. The combination of more colourful decoration and sober, traditional designs was in accord with European taste at this time. As a result, craftwork from China became part of a growing trade with Europe, where a fascination of all things Chinese led to a flowering of Chinoiserie. The Manchus love of bright colours extended to court costume and the painting of their palaces.

By the nineteenth century, as the wealth and power of the state declined, the artistic culture of China lost much of its vitality. Painters and craftsmen became accustomed to supplying a rich but uninformed market. Decoration became heavy and much of the Chinese art found in English country houses dates from the end of the nineteenth century. However, pots such as the one featured in this tapestry have, as Kaffe Fassett says, a 'rawness' which can work very well when used decoratively. Combined with the softer peony pinks and the dove grey background the cushion has a vibrancy which is only made possible with the yellows and turquoises from the original pot. It is also a good example of how a very bold, graphic design does not look overbearing when worked mainly in pale pastel colours. In fact the scale of the jar is part of the success of this design and it makes a very luxurious-looking cushion to sink into.

Variations

The four large peonies could be used on their own, either grouped in the centre or positioned at the corners, as in the original, but enlarged to fill most of the design area. Choose a textured stitch, such as rice stitch (page 64) or flat stitch for a solid colour background, perhaps in pale grey.

Flat stitch is quick to work and has an attractive, satiny effect. The square can be worked in alternating directions, as shown, or all in the same direction. The stitch is normally worked over four horizontal and vertical canvas threads, but its length can be adjusted to suit the design.

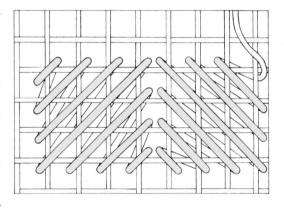

A simple way to enlarge a motif given in chart form is to work a square four stitches for each square indicated on the chart. If the same gauge canvas is used, the work will be twice as wide and twice as deep as the original. Alternatively, substitute one cross stitch (page 13) for each half-cross stitch (or box) on the chart.

If you are using this method – and so following the charts given for the peony motifs, rather than tracing and enlarging as described on page 7 – you will need to take some care in positioning the motifs. If you are adapting the design and using, for instance, a peony at each corner, begin at one corner, placing the peony about 3cm (1½in) from the edge of the worked area, and complete one whole peony; then position the others in relation to the first. If you are grouping them at the centre, decide on the grouping, then label each peony on the chart 'upper left', 'lower right', and so on. Mark the centre of the canvas and work each motif outwards from the centre.

This cushion would go extremely well with the fabrics and wallpapers Kaffe Fassett has designed for Designers' Guild. As with all Kaffe Fassett's needlepoints, the skill lies in part in his asymmetrical use of motifs. All four peonies are different. A less experienced designer would have made them regular and the design would have looked flat.

COLOURWAYS FOR PEONY JAR

An0402 (PA260) *a*

An0123 (PA341) *b*

An0429 (PA902) *c*

An0903 (PA750) *d*

An0325 (PA800) *e*

An067 (PA933) *f*

An0426 (PA802) *g*

An0167 (PA523) *h*

An0264 (PA653) *i*

An0144 (PA564) *j*

An0366 (PA805) *k*

An = Anchor
PA = Paterna

Yarn amounts

a	40m	(44yd)
b	15m	(17yd)
c	10m	(11yd)
d	10m	(11yd)
e	10m	(11yd)
f	25m	(28yd)
g	10m	(11yd)
h	20m	(22yd)
i	20m	(22yd)
j	30m	(33yd)
k	15m	(17yd)

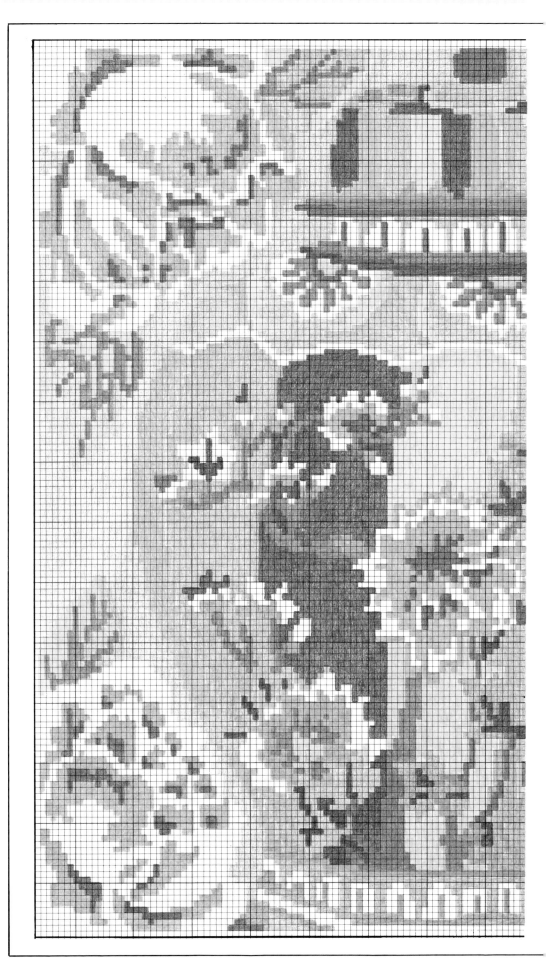

Materials
Tapestry wool (see colourways). The amounts given are calculated for half-cross stitch. To work the design in basketweave or continental tent, increase all amounts by 50 per cent. If either of these stitches is used, an ordinary mono canvas may be substituted for double thread or interlock. Three strands of Persian wool or four strands of crewel can be substituted for the single strand of tapestry wool used for this design.
10-gauge double or mono interlock canvas
    50cm (20in) square
Size 18 tapestry needle
50cm (20in) furnishing fabric for backing
1.8m (6ft) narrow piping cord
Cushion 40cm (16in) square
35cm (14in) zip fastener (optional)
Slate or stretcher frame (optional)
Tools and materials for preparing canvas
    (see page 10) and for blocking

The finished cushion measures approximately 40cm (16in) square.

Working the embroidery
Prepare the canvas and mount it on the frame, if used (see page 10). Following the chart on the left, work the design in half-cross stitch (or basketweave or continental tent stitch).

Blocking and making up
Block the completed work (see page 11) and allow it to dry thoroughly. Trim the canvas edges, leaving margins of 2cm (¾in).
    From the backing fabric cut a piece 44cm (17½in) square. Or, if inserting a zip, cut two pieces as specified on page 16.
    From the remaining fabric, cut and join bias strips to cover the piping cord (see page 48). Make up the piping.
    If using, insert the zip in the back cover (see page 16).
    Attach the piping to the back cover as described on page 48.
    Join the front and back covers as described on page 16, and insert the cushion.

Esphahan Rose

Kaffe Fassett once visited a school in Esphahan, in Persia, and found himself confronted by a huge expanse of roses: the walls of the school had been decorated entirely with painted tiles, each of them featuring a rose.

'It was an amazing sight. Roses, especially roses in an Eastern setting, will always bring back the memory of Esphahan, hence the name of this design, although it was inspired by a Persian carpet.

'I love roses and the timelessness of them. In this design I particularly liked the combination of the primitive carpet border and the more romantic treatment of the central rose. I have also worked this with a black background, which is very effective.'

Variations

The central rose motif would adapt well to use on a round footstool. First plan the size of the work by measuring the diameter of the footstool pad. To enlarge the motif, you will need to work four stitches for every square on the chart; using this as a basis, calculate the gauge of canvas required (described on page 6). Mark the chosen centre of the motif on the chart, and mark the centre of the canvas. Work the embroidery starting from the centre and working outwards.

You could also use the rose motif for a round cushion. Use the method described above for adjusting the size, and make up the cushion as described on page 16.

The border of this design could be adapted for use as a picture or mirror frame. Notice that each segment of the border is slightly different from the others, which adds to the charm of the design. To adapt it for a frame, you will, of course, need to plan the areas now occupied by the spotted cream background. You could keep this design, but work the background in the cocoa brown. Or you could work it in a solid colour, picking up one of the colours in the floral part of the border.

The design could also be used for a rug – in keeping with its original inspiration. Repeat the design to make a rug of the required size, using 7- or 8-gauge canvas and rug wool or Persian wool. Make up the rug as described on page 108.

A typical Fassett design combining two of his favourite themes: oriental rug patterning and flowers. The border is tricky, with numerous colour changes dotted all over. The cushion is shown here on a pale background to bring out the subtle colouring of the roses. Note Kaffe Fassett's totally unexpected choice of peppermint green for the leaves.

Materials

Tapestry wool (see colourways). The amounts given are calculated for half-cross stitch. To work the design in basketweave or continental tent, increase all amounts by 50 per cent. If either of these stitches is used, an ordinary mono canvas may be substituted for double thread or interlock. Two strands of Persian wool or three strands of crewel can be substituted for the single strand of tapestry wool used for this design.

10-gauge canvas 40cm (16in) square
Size 18 tapestry needle
40cm furnishing fabric for backing
1.4m (4½ft) narrow piping cord
Cushion 30cm (12in) square
25cm (10in) zip fastener (optional)
Slate or stretcher frame (optional)
Tools and materials for preparing canvas
    (see page 10) and for blocking (page 11).

The finished cushion measures 30cm (12in) square.

Working the embroidery

Prepare the canvas and mount it on the frame, if used (see page 10). Following the chart on the right, work the design in half-cross stitch (or basketweave or continental tent stitch).

Blocking and making up

Block the completed work (see page 11) and allow it to dry thoroughly. Trim the canvas edges, leaving margins of 2cm (¾in).

From the backing fabric cut a piece 34cm (13½in) square. Or, if inserting a zip, cut two pieces as specified on page 16.

From the remaining fabric, cut and join bias strips to cover the piping cord (see page 48). Make up the piping.

Insert the zip, if using, in the back cover.

Attach the piping to the back cover as described on page 48.

Join the front and back covers as described on page 16, and insert the cushion.

COLOURWAYS FOR ESPHAHAN ROSE

An0386 (PA263)	*a*	
An0351 (PA870)	*b*	
An0983 (PD123)	*c*	
An0147 (PA502)	*d*	
An0412 (PA831)	*e*	
An0895 (PA904)	*f*	
An0242 (PA613)	*g*	
An0837 (PA525)	*h*	
An0311 (PA703)	*i*	
An0893 (PA946)	*j*	

An = Anchor
PA or PD = Paterna

Yarn amounts

a	50m	(55yd)
b	20m	(22yd)
c	30m	(33yd)
d	10m	(11yd)
e	10m	(11yd)
f	20m	(22yd)
g	10m	(11yd)
h	20m	(22yd)
i	20m	(22yd)
j	20m	(22yd)

Baroda Stripe

Inspired by the patterning of tribal rugs, this design has the wavy lines characteristic of woven rugs from the Caucasus. In this area, during the second half of the nineteenth century, cottage weavers became very inventive, reworking traditional patterns woven from memory or with the aid of a drawing. These rugs are now much in demand with collectors and general public alike. In complete contrast to the Persian city-style carpet, they have a pleasing irregularity and 'guts' associated with hand-woven items. They have strong, bright colours and a naïvety of execution which gives the rug an enduring freshness.

Kaffe Fassett's designs are often inspired by Oriental carpets or Islamic patterns and they retain that asymmetrical roughness which gives life and vitality to all old textiles. His unique sense of colour, whether in warm autumnal tones or faded pastels, transforms these designs into instantly recognizable Kaffe Fassett tapestries.

Variations

The border design of the cushion could easily be used for an attractive belt. You can begin anywhere along the border you wish and work the motifs in any sequence until the belt is the length you want. Choose either of the striped narrow edgings, or work plain edgings in a single colour.

The complete design, repeated and worked on rug canvas, would make a handsome rug. You should use a slightly coarser canvas than the 10-gauge used for the cushion; if you are using an 8-gauge rug canvas, you will need a piece of canvas at least 100cm wide by 145cm long (40×58in) to accommodate six repeats. See page 108 for instructions on making up a rug.

OTHER IDEAS

Attaching a backing

A flat item, such as a rug, belt or coaster, must be backed or lined with some suitable material. A non-fraying material such as leather – real or synthetic – or felt is often ideal, since the edges need not be turned under, and in some cases can simply be glued to the back of the work.

Turn under and steam-press the unworked canvas edges, first trimming them to an appropriate depth: 2cm (1in) or less for a coaster; 4cm (1½in) for a rug.

If your canvas is circular, cut notches out of the turned-under canvas to allow it to lie flat. Apply iron-on interfacing cut to fit before attaching the lining.

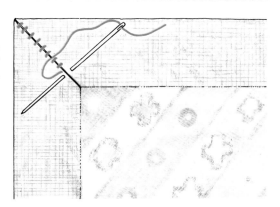

On a rectangular canvas, mitre the corners. Press the canvas diagonally over the corner, then cut away a small square as shown, leaving a few canvas threads at the corner. Then fold the edges to meet in the centre and oversew together firmly. If working on a rug, oversew the edges to the back of the work to hold them in place.

Cut the lining to fit, adding extra for turnings, if necessary. Press under any turnings, mitring the corners, then hand-stitch the lining in place, using small oversewing stitches, or slipstitch; or stick it down with fabric glue.

A cushion with the feel of kelim carpets. Kaffe Fassett's cushion patterns are almost always worked on 10-mesh canvas to give life rather than detail to the design, and you should never try to straighten up an edge or make a line neater!

**COLOURWAYS
FOR BARODA
STRIPE**

An0386 (PA263) *a*

An0983 (PA123) *b*

An0147 (PA502) *c*

An0339 (PA722) *d*

An0347 (PD423) *e*

An0159 (PA505) *f*

An0566 (PD503) *g*

An0305 (PA763) *h*

An0892 (PA492) *i*

An = Anchor
PA or PD = Paterna

Yarn amounts

a	20m	(22yd)
b	30m	(33yd)
c	20m	(22yd)
d	20m	(22yd)
e	20m	(22yd)
f	20m	(22yd)
g	20m	(22yd)
h	20m	(22yd)
i	20m	(22yd)

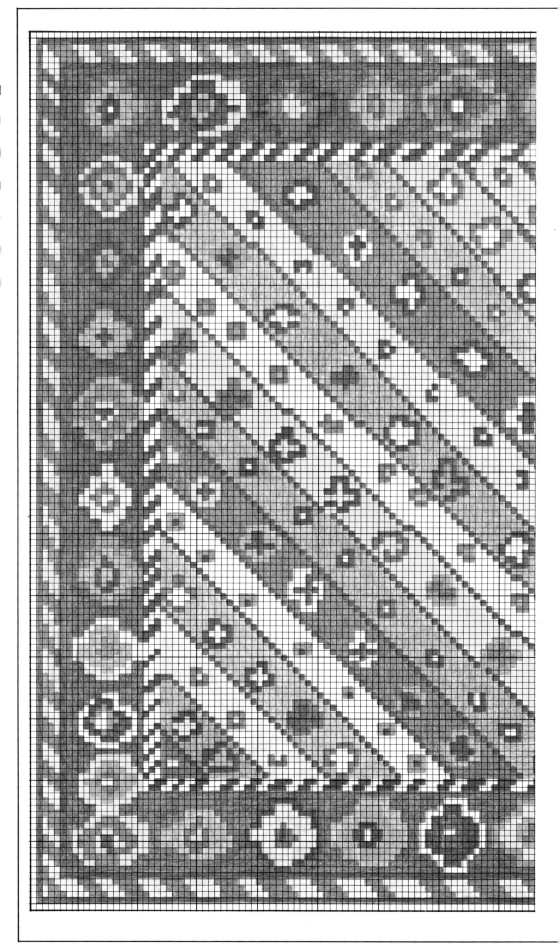

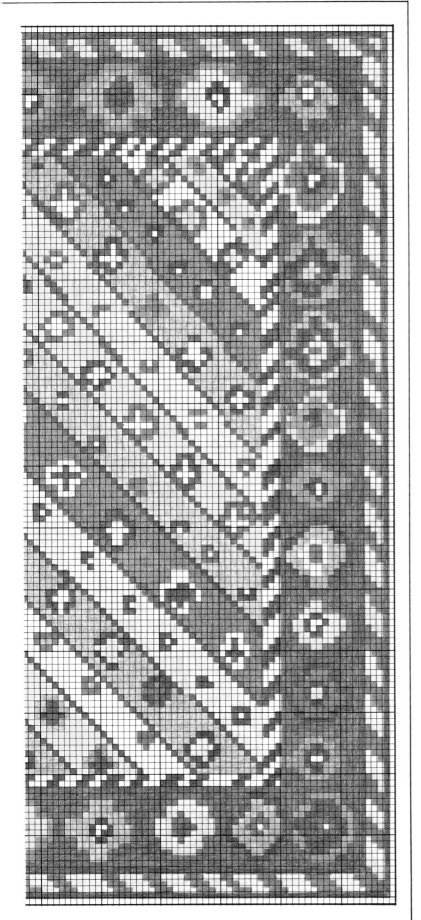

Materials
Tapestry wool (see colourways). The amounts given are calculated for half-cross stitch. To work the design in basketweave or continental tent, increase all amounts by 50 per cent. If either of these stitches is used, an ordinary mono canvas may be substituted for double thread or interlock. Three strands of Persian wool or four strands of crewel can be substituted for the single strand of tapestry wool used for this design.
10-gauge double or mono interlock canvas
    45cm (18in) square
Size 18 tapestry needle
40cm (16in) furnishing fabric for backing
1.5m (5ft) narrow piping cord
Cushion 35cm (14in) or 38cm (15in)
    square
30cm (12in) zip fastener (optional)
Slate or stretcher frame (optional)
Tools and materials for preparing canvas
    (see page 10) and for blocking (page 11).

The finished cushion measures approximately 35cm (14in) square.

Working the embroidery
Prepare the canvas and mount it on the frame, if used (see page 10).
    Following the chart on the left, work the design in half-cross stitch (or basketweave or continental tent stitch).

Blocking and making up
Block the completed work (see page 11) and allow it to dry thoroughly. Trim the canvas edges, leaving margins of 2cm (¾in).
    From the backing fabric cut a piece 39cm (15½in) square. Or, if inserting a zip, cut two pieces as specified on page 16.
    From the remaining fabric, cut and join bias strips to cover the piping cord (see page 48). Make up the piping.
    Insert the zip, if used, in the back cover.
    Attach the piping to the back cover as described on page 48.
    Join the front and back covers as described on page 16, and insert the cushion.

ACKNOWLEDGEMENTS

Special thanks to Gillian Meakin at William Briggs & Co. for organizing design origination; to Jack Crease and John Armitage of Appleton Bros. for so promptly supplying all the yarns; to Hilda and Sue at the shop for coping with it all; to David Rutter at Vicars & Poirson Ltd, who produced our first kit; and a very general thank you to Judy Brittain, Elizabeth Pettifer, Kaffe Fassett and Richard Womersley, Maggie Stevenson, Elizabeth Benn and Edwin Belchamber for their invaluable help and encouragement with our tapestries over the years.

We would like to thank, too, the following companies for their help:

Heals, for supplying the vases shown on pp 14-15, 45, 111, 114;

Robert and Colleen Bery for the tray on p 111, the panels on pp 45 and 71, the wooden fan on pp 18-19, the coffee table on p 45, and the box on p 93.

Material Effects, London SW7, for the fabric on pp 14-15, 18-19, 25, 28, 45, 56-7, 84, 85, 93, 111 and 123, and Marlene Adcock for the vase on pp 56-7;

Sue Wales for the painting on p 111;

Hackett, London SW6, for the canes on p 40;

Sandra Wall (The Stable Gallery, London SW18) for the watercolour on p 50;

Designers' Guild for the fabric on pp 93, 104.

Flowers throughout supplied by Honeysuckle, Bellevue Road, London SW18.

ORDER FORM FOR KITS

Needlepoint kits

The designs listed on the right are available as kits containing the printed canvas, needle, instructions and enough pure wool yarn to complete the design in half-cross or continental stitch.

The footstool kits also contain a polished mahogany footstool with a detachable calico-covered top to which the tapestry is attached, and instructions on how to do this. The chair seat comes with enough background wool to cover an area 50cm square (20×20in), and extra hanks may be ordered.

How to order

1. All postage and packing charges are included in the stated price for kits despatched within the United Kingdom.
2. Make your cheque or postal order payable to Ehrman Kits Ltd. Send your order to Designer Needlepoint Kits at the address below (no stamp is needed).
3. Overseas: for all kits sent abroad, excluding USA and Canada, add £2 per kit.
4. USA and Canada: orders should be sent to: Hugh Ehrman, 5 Northern Boulevard, Amherst, North Hampshire, 03031 USA.

Terms

Delivery normally within 28 days. Money back if kit returned unused within 14 days. If you have any enquiries on kit deliveries please ring 01-937 4568.

Page	Design	Price
123	Baroda Stripe	£19.95
29	Butterfly footstool	£34.50
29	Butterfly tapestry	£16.95
93	Carnation: Blue	£19.95
93	Carnation: Ivory	£19.95
54	Chintz: Blue	£19.95
50	Chintz: Pink	£19.95
35	Chippendale Rose	£19.95
97	Elephant	£19.95
119	Esphahan Rose	£19.95
28	Floral footstool	£34.50
28	Floral tapestry	£16.95
56	Fox and Crane	£19.95
100	Harvesters	£19.95
25	Honeysuckle chair seat: Blue	£23.50
25	Honeysuckle chair seat: Green	£23.50
'84	Lily Pond	£19.95
40	Oakleaves and Acorns	£19.95
18	Paradise Bird	£19.95
114	Peony Jar	£19.95
100	Reapers	£19.95
64	Red House	£17.95
111	Seabird	£19.95
78	Seashore Garland	£16.95
75	Shells	£19.95
71	Three Birds	£19.95
60	Turkish Stripe	£22.00
45	Urns and Fruit	£19.95
104	Vase Rug	£49.50
18	Victorian Bird	£19.95
85	Walled Garden	£19.95
100	Winemakers	£19.95

To: Designer Needlepoint Kits, Ehrman, Freepost, London, W8 4BR

Please use BLOCK CAPITALS

From: (Name) _____

Address: _____

_____

Design	Kit No.	Quantity	Price

Total: _____